THE FOURTH WAY TO NOWHERE

The fourth way to nowhere

The search for cosmic consciousness and the triumph of the ordinary

A quest for the meaning of life,
a critical analysis of the teaching of Gurdjieff and Ouspensky,
and my twenty-seven-year membership of a fourth way cult

Martin Braybrooke

Narrow Gate Press
London MMXXI

Thema category codes: QRYC, QRYA, VXA, JBSX

ISBN: 978-0-9565497-8-5

Published by Narrow Gate Press,
BM Box 6798, London WC1N 3XX

www.ngp.co

PREFACE

My father was by turns a Quaker, a Catholic and a Buddhist, my mother an atheist, and my primary school teacher believed that her dog was the reincarnation of her previous dog. Thus I grew up a natural skeptic. It is odd, therefore, that I ended up believing a large number of the unprovable fragments of an unknown teaching that is the fourth way.

This book is a careful critique of a whole set of beliefs related to, but not exclusive to, the fourth way path of inner development. At the same time it is a personal history of how the author, despite a modern education, got drawn into a cult, and believed (to quote the White Queen in *Alice*), at least 'six impossible things before breakfast.'

Those readers already familiar with the fourth way, and perhaps even members of one or other of the organisations that have sprung up in connection with it, should find the analysis in these pages useful and perhaps challenging. There are indeed ideas in the fourth way worth considering, not least the idea of self-remembering, which has a lot in common with more recent movements such as mindfulness. There are other ideas which are questionable, or remain to be proven, such as the fourth state of consciousness or the idea of recurrence: Ouspensky's version of re-incarnation. No genuine seeker after truth should be deterred from asking her- or himself, "what do I really know, what is merely provisional, and what is likely to turn out to be wrong?"

This is also a plea that one aim of any spiritual or psychological practice or movement should be kindness, if humanity is to survive the various catastrophes that now threaten it, and an assertion that aspirants to self-development can arrive, with the right efforts, at a place where it is no small achievement to be content to be ordinary.

ACKNOWLEDGEMENTS

I am indebted to my long-time friend John Dewey Jones with whom many of these ideas have been discussed, and who has diligently read the manuscript several times, both mercilessly critiquing the ideas and at the same time pointing out infelicities of prose. This book would be a lot poorer without his input. Any remaining errors, whether philosophical or textual are the responsibility of the author.

I am also grateful to all those in my family who have put up with me, whether because of my membership of a fourth way cult or otherwise.

WORKS REFERRED TO

As Alice might have said, "What is the use of a book without footnotes?" Details of the works referred to are in the footnotes and in the bibliography at the end.

Contents

THE AROUSING OF THOUGHT

"Oh, I've had such a curious dream!" said Alice ...[1]

One day it became clear to me that I no longer believed in the cult of which I had been a member for twenty-seven years. In some respects this parting of the ways had been coming for a long time. In other ways it was almost a surprise to me.

I had joined with the belief that here was a teaching, perhaps ancient, which could lead to higher states of consciousness, which could lead one back to one's own birthright as a human being. I came disillusioned from the peace movement, with the strong feeling that no amount of political protest was going to save humanity from itself, and with the conviction that the only way forward was inner transformation—to start with myself, perhaps to help others to do the same.

Thus began my journey from what still seem to me reasonable grounds, into a cult in which the ideas of Ouspensky's and Gurdjieff's fourth way were transformed into something different, and in which there was a smell of corruption which others had smelled long before I joined, but which I did not smell until I left.

I cannot fully verify the corruption. I faithfully followed the task set by the Teacher not to read the on-line blog in which ex-members vent, complain and catalogue abuse, only reading it after I had decided to leave. I feel some guilt that I stayed so long, supporting with regular donations what turned out to be an elaborate deception.

I shall not assert anything that is not within my experience, and I write only what I myself felt, saw and heard while I was a member. Plenty of material is available to

---

[1] Lewis Carroll, *Alice's Adventures in Wonderland*, ch. 12

anyone from an easy internet search.[2] I am however nauseated at what I have read and keep asking myself why I did not ask questions when cracks appeared in the elegant façade of the school.

This is my version of the truth, from twenty-seven years in a particular fourth way school, the so-called *Fellowship of Friends*.[3]

I did not live in the California headquarters, variously named Renaissance, Apollo, Isis (after the Egyptian goddess and with no connection with the notorious terrorist organisation of that name) and again Apollo, but I visited it a few times and met the Teacher on many occasions both in Apollo and in London. I was for most of my membership a regular attender at the London Centre, once or twice a week, and visited a number of centres worldwide. At one time I was a Centre Director in London.

This is my attempt to understand how I came to believe things that now seem to me absurd, to look critically at the elements of the fourth way as practised in the School, and to clarify what remains in the fourth way that is of genuine value. There are a few gems to pick out of the dirt.

Here are some of the questions I shall try to address in what follows. What is living well? And is there a path to living well in which belief plays the smallest possible part? Do we ever live without belief, or do we simply change one belief for another?

Is there such a thing as cosmic consciousness and what can it tell us about the world we live in? To what extent do we need a teacher to guide us, when do we need to abandon the teacher, and how can we tell a true teacher from a false? When does practice end and play begin?

Is there, at the heart of everything, in the soul of every true religion or just in ourselves, independent of any belief

---

[2] https://robertearlburton.blogspot.com/

[3] No connection with the Society of Friends (Quakers).

system, a still, small voice and a way of getting to that place of inner peace? And crucially, is this a purely selfish pursuit or, as I believed, something of value to others, as if one's own pursuit of peace might spread peace?

CULT VERSUS BELIEF

Do not build a Dervish convent or live in one.
—Abdulhalik Gudjduvani[4]

How does a cult differ from any guiding belief? Having been in a cult and come out, I am re-examining what it is I know and what I merely believed.

I was looking for meaning in life, and for twenty-seven years I was a member of what some would call a cult, others a fourth way school—the Fellowship of Friends led by its teacher Robert Earl Burton ('the Teacher'). Over the years many have left. Many students remain, for the most part beautiful and sincere people. (How people who are beautiful and sincere also appeared to receive with equanimity the Teacher's prediction that California would fall into the sea and millions of non-cult members drown is an important question. I also wonder about those at the centre of the school who must know exactly what is going on.)

Now I have dropped out. I have read the testimonies of other ex-students, testimonies I had not read before. Some, according to their accounts, were sexually abused and damaged. Some have merely spent a large part of their incomes and others wasted years when they might have been happier doing something else. I cannot speak for them.

For myself, I have mixed feelings: I have given twelve percent of my after-tax income, yet I have done well enough. I did not live at Apollo on a below-minimum wage while the world passed me by. I did not abandon my 'life' family. I did not entirely abandon my skepticism, but I did

---

4 Shushud, *Masters of Wisdom of Central Asia*, p.30

compartmentalise it (perhaps that is the most interesting part of coming to believe unverifiable things—how a scientifically-educated person can be fooled—or fool themselves). By applying some of the methods of the fourth way, I have learned things that still seem to me of value that perhaps I might not have learned any other way. Yet even that is a difficult claim to verify. How much might I have learned simply by looking after my family and doing my job with persistence and sincerity?

Like it or not we all need a world view to live by. That world view may be as narrow as self-centred self-interest which ricochets like a pin-ball from one event to the next, or as wide as Jesus's philosophy of love or Buddha's middle way. But it is impossible to live without some guiding principles, even if they are just money, sex and beer. Whatever I arrive at will undoubtedly be simpler and humbler than what I had before.

There is a quotation I came across to the effect that young men come to Athens to learn wisdom, but when they get there they learn to be ordinary.[5] I have learned at any rate that there is nothing wrong with being ordinary, as long as you do it properly.

THE ARCH-ABSURD

Alice laughed. "There's no use trying," she said: "one can't believe impossible things."
"I daresay you haven't had much practice," said the Queen. "When I was your age, I always did it for half-an-hour a day. Why, sometimes I've believed as many as six impossible things before breakfast."[6]

How did I come to believe so many doubtful and even unprovable things?

---

[5] I have been unable to locate the source of this quotation. I think I may have read it in Plutarch.

[6] Lewis Carroll, Through the Looking Glass, chapter 5

Forty-four invisible conscious beings—angels—watching over our School and its students. They signal to us in co-incidences, messages on billboards and car licence plates (the interpretation of which is largely by the Teacher, although sometimes by us in imitation of him). Past conscious beings have encoded the secrets of awakening not only in scriptures but in the bridge in the background of the Mona Lisa, in the square trouser leg of Diego Rivera's self-portrait, and in potsherds and wall-paintings from Neolithic times. The spirit of Leonardo da Vinci, an ascended conscious being, guides our Teacher. Students will become permanently conscious in our ninth lifetimes (and we are mostly on our eighth). If we do not develop a permanent tendency to awaken (or lose the School) we shall become food for the moon. The School is an ark for the preservation of civilisation from a coming catastrophe, variously the fall of California and nuclear war. At one time I believed all this, more or less.

In fairness to the fourth way of Gurdjieff and Ouspensky, the Fellowship deviated more and more from the original teaching. Later I shall give a brief overview of the history and fundamental teachings of the fourth way, before looking at the ideas in more detail, trying to separate the plausible from the bizarre.

Robert Burton frequently said that he did not innovate but was merely uncovering what had been hidden, newly revealed to him by Influence C. However the idea of Influence C as 'angels,' the idea of nine lifetimes and most recently the Sequence are all innovations not present in the basic texts of Ouspensky and Gurdjieff. The most egregious innovation, and the one that was the final straw for me, was the claim that in 2018 the Absolute had personally visited Robert in the rose garden.

Question: I cannot recapture the faith of my childhood.
Gurdjieff: That is not necessary. You have lost that possibility. You are no longer a child, you are big now. You should have logic and not

search automatically. To have direct contact with God is impossible. Millions and millions of nonentities wish to have relations with Mr God direct. This is impossible.[7]

No doubt apologists for Mr Burton would say that Mr Burton is not a non-entity at all, but is special: as he himself claims, a goddess in a man's body. However Ouspensky said that the Absolute cannot interact directly with humans:

...it is impossible for the will of the Absolute to enter our level. In order to do that the Absolute would have to destroy all the intermediate worlds, since everything depends on the laws governing them.[8]

...and Robert Burton once agreed:

Mr Gurdjieff said the Absolute's influence does not reach us directly, and he is correct. Influence C help us. We do not need God—the Absolute—he is too big for us and has more important matters to attend to.[9]

The fourth way begins with some verifiable observations and some plausible ideas. With Ouspensky it merges into the tacit acceptance of the speculative and unverifiable, and in the Fellowship to the utterly fantastical.

As a child sometimes for fun I would walk on a wall which, because of a slope in the pavement would start close to the ground, but by the other end was too high to jump down from without getting hurt. In such a way a plausible idea is added to in small increments, until one is very far from any kind of solid ground.

So how did I get to the wrong end of the wall?

---

[7] Transcripts of Gurdjieff's Meetings 1941-46, p.106.

[8] Fourth Way p.194

[9] Self Remembering, p.159

How I came to be in an esoteric school: SES

When I was thirteen years old I formed in my mind and heart the very definite intention to find out the meaning of life. That was how I expressed it to myself then. I remember exactly where I was at the time, at the top of the school playing fields during a break.

The possibility that it has no meaning other than what we give it had not occurred to me, or if I had come across such an idea, I dismissed it. Some years later I remember a teacher at university pouring scorn on the idea of wanting to know the meaning of life, regarding it as simply a naïve phase of youth that people grow out of. For my part I regarded that attitude in turn as simply the ignorant fossilisation of old age.[10]

Maybe it was because my life had been quite painful at times and I felt there must be something better, but it was at a time in my life when for me things were actually going quite well. The most miserable year of my life was when I was ten years old, and this was not noticed by my parents, however they had other things on their minds. But by thirteen I was settled and thriving in a school that I loved and had a friend from the age of twelve with whom I have kept in touch ever since. Despite the impending breakup of my parents' marriage this was in some ways one of the happiest times of my life.

During the same year I had been reading Lao Tzu and I associate this in my mind with a moment of presence in the town centre. I remember exactly where I was and what I was looking at. It was merely the wall of a building near the Town Hall. The moment lasted only a few seconds. I remember trying to get it back but I didn't know how. I now know that there is work that can be done to make such states possible,

---

[10] "This unlearned person grows up like an ox. His bulk increases, his wisdom increases not." Buddha, trans. Carter and Palihawadana, *Dhammapada*, Oxford University Press, 1992, p.38.

yet often nothing happens, and then some other time it is given to you, out of the blue. It is like the Christian idea of work and grace. You try, then learn not to try, then it comes.

The balance between what in the Christian tradition is called work and faith was important to me. I did not expect that simply believing something (and particularly something impossible to verify) would somehow lead to salvation. Somewhere Gurdjieff compares this to standing with your mouth open expecting a cooked chicken to fly into it. I was looking for a method, a way.

Another influence was that the head teacher used to read a passage from the New Testament every morning in assembly. There can't have been more than half a dozen passages that he would read from. For this reason, without intending to I memorised some of them. Even though I had become an atheist from the age of ten (when I felt that there could not be a God, partly because of the misery I was then in) those passages have stuck with me.

At the age of about sixteen or seventeen I met a friend of my mother's who was involved in the School of Economic Science (SES). By then I had already heard of Ouspensky and Gurdjieff and read Ouspensky's *Tertium Organum* (which I asked for as a school prize —I still have it); I do not recall when I read *In Search of the Miraculous*, it may have been much later. In any event this lady informed me that there was indeed a School and so I attended the introductory lectures. I used to hitch-hike up to London to do so, and later on was enabled to stay over at a family's house and hitch back the following morning.

The SES advertises itself as a school of practical philosophy, but its history connects it with Ouspensky via Dr Francis Roles and his friendship with SES leader Leon MacLaren. At the time I joined, it had located a teacher in India, the Shankaracharya of the North, and the philosophy taught was very much connected with the art of presence, combining a Sanskrit terminology with neo-Platonic ideas from the Italian Renaissance.

The exercise is something that was taught in the SES in the first or one of the first introductory meetings. One sits and becomes aware of all one's sensations, the weight of the body on the chair, the sensation of air on the face, the sounds in and outside the room, any visual impressions in the room.

The exercise, done in a conducive atmosphere, brings one into the present and lets worries drop away. One can with practice learn to be in something like this state in more-or-less any situation, although in my experience at first the automatic flow of worries and associations makes efforts of this kind very difficult. Mostly one just forgets. If one remembers it is for brief intervals, and the effort sometimes feels like wading through treacle. With repeated efforts one can reach this state more easily, and lot of unnecessary preoccupations either dissolve or are seen in context as less important.

I continued attending after going up to university and joined the youth group, which met and worked at Waterperry House in Oxfordshire alternate weekends. Waterperry House is a large country manor house, the front of which is 18th century in an austere style, and the back is older. In those days it had not yet been redecorated inside or adorned with the colourful philosophical murals it now has in the centre. It was also cold.

I used to cycle there through country lanes. I often got chased by dogs and was once bitten on the way. Most of the others came up in a coach from London. We would stay overnight in rudimentary conditions in the attic. By day the young men would usually work in the grounds, which had once been a horticultural college, and the young women would work in lighter garden duties or in the kitchen. We were assumed to be equal, but at that time the SES had an ethos that the sexes were each more suited to particular roles. After cleaning away the garden tools, which were washed, oiled and each hung in place, we would listen to music played on the piano by one of the youth group members who could play Mozart very well. Another student could sing Purcell's Music for a While from the poem by John Dryden, which is the perfect thing to listen to when you have a mind tense with anxiety:

> Music for a while
> Shall all your cares beguile.
> Wond'ring how your pains were eas'd
> And disdaining to be pleas'd
> Till Alecto free the dead
> From their eternal bands,
> Till the snakes drop from her head,
> And the whip from out her hands.
> Music for a while
> Shall all your cares beguile.

Then we would go in to dinner, which was simple but nourishing. Afterwards there would be washing up and the boiling of linen.

Sometimes senior students and Leon MacLaren himself would be there, but apart from helping prepare their food and wash up afterwards we did not mix with them. They had a special diet which consisted of fruit, honey, bread and cheese, and when Mr MacLaren was present there would be Nuits-St-Georges red wine also. I was once given a part-filled glass to taste and I was amazed, not merely by the fact that that small amount would have been very expensive but also by the fact that it tasted like a piece of heaven.

While working we would make efforts to put the attention on the point where the working surfaces met. This was exactly what I had been looking for: a method. There were also talks, most of which I have forgotten, but once we were given a brief talk by Leon MacLaren's father Andrew MacLaren, then in his 90s, who lectured us about land value taxation (I seem to recall something about being asked to 'fight for your country' in World War One and MacLaren senior, according to his own report, pointing out that he didn't own as much of his country as was in a flower pot). We also had talks from Leon MacLaren occasionally and were once introduced to Dr Roles, although I don't remember what if anything he said to us. I think it was Andrew MacLaren who told us we were all 'stuffed shirts.' The other youth group that met alternate weekends were considered to be more like hippies.

I was not good at mixing with people, and in particular I failed to attract a girlfriend, my other abiding passion at the time, but nevertheless I found a certain peace there. The youth group leader, Mr N. was a friendly avuncular man. He once quoted to me from Gilbert and Sullivan, 'a most intense young man, conceive me if you can,' as a gentle and no doubt accurate observation of how I was. Once he asked me, 'how's the tiny?'—meaning, the tiny mind. I did not in the least take offence at this—clearly he did not intend an insult. Rather it was a way of helping me out of the foggy and slightly tormented mental state that I was habitually in. 'The tiny' referred to the classification of mind in Vedanta (as taught in SES at that time) as *manas*, the monkey mind. Above that is *buddhi*[11]—some kind of higher mind, a concept I did not fully understand. However, that the monkey mind is not us, that it is possible to be other than its continuous chatter, is a topic that I shall return to.

One time we were listening to a recording of a performance of Leon MacLaren's oratorio, text based on Isaiah. This is actually a beautiful work, and I have never heard it performed since (other than a single performance at St Augustine's church, Kensington) nor seen any trace of it at

---

[11] *Buddhi* is derived from the Vedic Sanskrit root *Budh* which literally means "to wake, be awake, observe, heed, attend, learn, become aware of, to know, be conscious again" Cited in Wikipedia from the Sanskrit dictionary of Monier-Williams et al.

SES events.[12] There were one or two wrong notes, after all, it was an amateur choir, and some of us winced a bit. Mr N. told us to listen to the good. We were focusing on the wrong things. This does not mean there were not imperfections, rather that in paying too much attention to the imperfections and our own reactions to them we were missing the larger beauty. I am convinced that this is a powerful technique to deal with many things in life.

One weakness, I think, of the earlier introductory lectures in London, or perhaps it was a weakness in me, was the impression that full *realisation* as a human being (whatever that was) was just around the corner. I suppose if you can get a medical degree in five or six years it's not totally unreasonable to suppose that you can get what the School offers in much the same time period. I did not then have the perspective I had subsequently, that to practise medicine really well you need not only post-graduate studies but also a lifetime of practising, and even then there is more to learn than any one person can ever know.

But then, what is *realisation*? Is there some kind of clarity of mind which leads to nirvana and the end of suffering? Some Zen koans relate stories of students achieving sudden realisation—at least for a moment—right now. Here is the paradox, or perhaps the central deception: pushing awakening into the future, when the only time available to us is now.

During my time in SES I was initiated into the meditation technique that was brought to the West by the Maharishi. One time during meditation I experienced something that has never entirely left me, although there have been many times when I have forgotten it. It was a state of no words and no thoughts—but nevertheless a conscious state—of perfect peace. I shall not attempt to describe it further now, as any

---

[12] A search reveals a 2013 recording: www.philosophybookshop.com/in-the-beginning

such attempt tends to lose it in mere words. Some part of me still seeks this.

As an undergraduate I came under the influence of my college tutor, and I still don't fully understand what happened. He was a strange and charismatic person, certainly he seemed to me a lot more serious and profound than many of the other people I met. This was a painful time in my life, when I had not really grown up. He said that the people at SES did not 'see' me—but I now think he did not 'see' me either. It would be an oversimplification to say that I was looking for a father-figure, because Mr N. who led the SES youth group answered that description much better. In any event, with the weak excuse that I needed more time for my studies I left SES after having been part of it for four years.

That decision was a wrench and provoked a storm of contradictory thoughts. I remember sitting in the college chapel on my own as the 'reasons' for staying or leaving went this way and that like a storm of flies. I now think the decision went the way it did because I had believed too many things. I think I had fallen in love with the teaching and the School, I was hungry for the knowledge that I had been seeking. Then when it was challenged by someone I respected I realised that many of the things I had accepted I could not justify. Some years later I drove to Waterperry just to look at the big house, somehow to assuage a sense of loss. I drove away again after a few minutes, knowing there was nothing there for me because I had left it.

I spent much of my life, then and since, looking for answers to the big questions, trying to construct philosophical theories of everything, which because I also discussed them with others were constantly being knocked down.

Had I read Ouspensky more thoroughly I might have understood that my problem with the SES was a mismatch between knowledge and being. I believed what I had been told, without having checked it against experience or any external standard. I swallowed the SES theory of the world whole, so that when one part of it was demolished the whole of it collapsed. I now think that the safest way to proceed is only to accept what you yourself have verified, and leave everything else an open question, but this is not easy. To look at it another way, knowledge that has not been verified is not really knowledge. It is dogma. There are good reasons for accepting dogma if you are learning a practical trade, but in the realm of science, and in any other search for truth, all dogma is provisional.

Before I leave the topic of the SES I have to point out that it is not hard to find stories of disaffected ex-students, and particularly stories of past abuse of children in schools associated with the SES.[13] I have not commented on this because I have no first-hand knowledge of it. There is only one anecdote that I can supply and it may or may not be representative. As a youth I used to stay overnight in an SES family's home to enable me to attend evening meetings in London. Their young daughter, who must have been about eight years old, maybe younger, was doing some homework consisting of calligraphy. One of the activities of the youth group was calligraphy, so I knew how we were supposed to sit, writing on paper on a raised easel, sitting straight, feet on the floor. The little girl was sitting slightly sideways with her feet swinging. I mentioned this to her parents, and one of them immediately struck the girl hard with a hand and made her cry. This shocked me and I wished I had said nothing.

Does dogmatism lead directly to cruelty? There is, in any case, a danger in any organisation or society that only accepts one way of interpreting the world and encourages no discussion outside the accepted view. This applies just as much to ordinary universities and schools and indeed

---

[13] http://www.ses-forums.org

ordinary families and individuals as it does to organisations that might be called cults.

IN SEARCH OF THE MIRACULOUS: THE FELLOWSHIP

Some nineteen years later I was working on a painting project that required great accuracy. I was painting a straight line. Suddenly, for reasons that are not clear and without looking up, I became aware of my surroundings other than just the paintbrush, and there seemed to be more light, although nothing in my surroundings had changed (I was actually in the garage). I put my attention on the point where the working surfaces met, as taught in the SES, and the line proceeded straight. A thought intruded, the feeling of presence was lost, and the line wavered also. Although this only lasted a few seconds, the thought then came, 'I must find people who know about this,' and that if necessary I would return to the SES and start all over again.

That is how I found the School. I had an old bookmark for 'Gurdjieff-Ouspensky Centres' in one of my books. I remember phoning all the numbers on it—some were dead, some had been reallocated. One of the last ones I tried was a number in California and it was just an answering machine. I left a message. Nothing happened for a few days. Then I was rung at about one o'clock in the morning and given the number of the London Centre. Then the line went dead, so I never found out who I had been speaking to.

The introductory meeting was in the Hampstead flat of a middle-aged couple on a long-term visit from the USA. Everything was very bright and neat. There was a gathering of maybe eight or ten students, some to give the meeting and some to observe, and eventually there were three of us as prospective students.

I already had high hopes before entering. I had been reading Ibn 'Arabi's Whoso knoweth himself,[14] a short book

---

[14] Ibn 'Arabi, Whoso knoweth himself, Beshara publications 1976

extracted from the *Treatise on Being*, the title based on a Hadith of Mohammed ('Whoso knoweth himself knoweth his Lord'). The book is a slim hardback volume, beautifully bound and with a gold geometric Kufic inscription on the cover. I felt I was on the verge of discovering something important, and the world seemed filled with light. Ibn 'Arabi argues that since there is only one God, everything is God, and he gets as close as he can to the claim of Vedanta that the real Self is God. Avoiding apparent heresy by a hair's breadth, he nevertheless claims that anything else is polytheism.

Entering the room I felt as though I were living in a fog and everyone else in the room was more there than I was. To walk across the room to deposit my coat felt like walking through illuminated space and I felt I was being observed. I hardly made eye-contact with anyone.

I imagine that my experience was part of my own subjectivity: I had already left my critical faculty behind. I also tend to be a shy person, not at ease in company, although this is something I have learned to overcome—not by becoming an extravert, which I was not born to be, but by learning that being present and listening to others puts me in a safe place from where I look out. In any event, my state of mind was clearly very different from that of the originator of the notorious blog many years later.[15]

Contrary to what is documented elsewhere, I did not find the people unfriendly or stand-off-ish. They asked us neither to believe nor disbelieve what we would hear, asked us to keep questions until tea was served, presented the material, and then served tea and biscuits. The idea that man is a sleeping machine and the possible levels of consciousness were explained, none of which I found surprising. The idea of self-remembering was introduced. There were two further meetings held a week apart. In these the body types and

---

[15] https://animamrecro.wordpress.com/2006/04/16/fellowship-of-friends-a-cult-for-intellectuals/

centres of gravity were explained (about all of which more later), and at the end also the conditions for joining including the payment and the no smoking rule. I do not remember asking any questions.

Of the three of us, two joined, and the other left after a few weeks, saying what he really wanted to know was the symbolism of Sufi carpets, which information was not available in the London Centre.

AN EARLY WARNING

Not too long after joining, a fellow student told me that one senior student in the early days of the school had given up her children in order to be with the Teacher. This struck me at the time as utterly incomprehensible.

This was told to me in the context of explaining how students at the beginning had to put up with far greater difficulties than we had to, in order to create the school. They had to live in very rudimentary conditions in order to establish the property at Renaissance (Apollo), for example. We who came later were the beneficiaries of their efforts, their payment for us.

I knew no details. I did not know whether Robert Burton had asked her to give up her children or whether he knew anything about it. She was not in the London Centre, and when I met her much later in my time in the school, it never seemed like an appropriate question to ask. There was no place for children in the early days of the school.

This alone should have been a warning to me. But I compartmentalised it as something I had no first-hand knowledge of. I was doing what the fourth way system itself calls 'buffering': the holding of incompatible beliefs simultaneously: not as possibilities without prejudice, but as beliefs sealed off from one another. This is sometimes referred to in non-esoteric circles as *cognitive dissonance*, in which the belief causing discomfort is ignored.[16]

Why did I not leave then? I think psychologically I was adrift, and as much committed by emotion as others are tied to the school by material factors. In some sense I had nowhere else to go. Curiously, when many years later I had decided to leave, I expressed my doubts to one of the Centre Directors at the time. He said he agreed with some of what I had said, but that he didn't leave because, he said, "It's the only game in town."

---

[16] Some years later, that student published a book in praise of Robert Burton, in which there is more detail as to what happened (Guinevere Ruth-Mueller, *Bread upon the water*, G&G Mueller, 1999). Her husband asked for a divorce a few months after she joined the School (p.8). "Robert had given an angle that children were an unnecessary law and the students had concluded that they did not wish to be under that law" (p.25). As a result of following Robert, she could not get a good job and the boys were not happy at school. Finally she signed over the care of the boys to her ex-husband. Shortly afterwards Robert asked her to move to Los Angeles to open a centre there, and the context implies that this was closer to where she could visit her boys (pp.50-51). Years later she entertained the boys, now young men, at the property. Robert told her, "Giving up your sons was a great sacrifice you made for our School" (p.52). To sacrifice means to make sacred (Latin *sacer* + *facere*). It would be up to the boys to know whether they had benefitted by being sacrificed.

THINGS THAT CAN BE TESTED

Basic ideas of the fourth way

The little essay that follows is a summary of the key elements of the fourth way.

Shortly before I left the School, but when I had already decided to leave, I was asked by a student at Apollo to write something for the London Centre Fourth Way Facebook page. I demurred, on the ground that I had very little to say. As my time in the School went on, I felt I knew less and less. I felt that many of the contributions of others were simply repeating old and stale material, much of which we had stopped working with long ago, and the Facebook page even mentioned J. G. Bennett and others with whom the Fellowship has no connection. If the School was about anything, it was about being present to each moment, it was about simplification in which the old stuff was no longer relevant. The student persisted, and I wrote the short essay reproduced here.

My intention was to write only what I felt I had verified. I wanted to emphasise the requirement of verification as a piece of clear advice to people who might join.

I also wanted to underline the concept of *good householder*, since I felt that in distancing themselves from their 'life' friends and 'life' family, students were in fact not in 'good householder' emotionally, and were also overlooking the fact that what distinguishes the fourth way from the other ways is that it takes place in ordinary life.

A life-long friend, not in the School, warned that this essay might on the contrary lull interested people into a false sense of security regarding the Fellowship. This was certainly a risk, however I felt it better stated than not. Perhaps it would also be a message for any existing students who had swapped verification for blind belief and might heed a wake-up call. In any event this little essay is now buried beneath other posts, as happens to things on social media.

WHAT IS THE FOURTH WAY?

Key ideas: the fourth way takes place in life—good householder—self-remembering—the non-expression of negative emotions—verification as a continuous process.

The fourth way is so called because it is not one of three other ways, the way of the monk, the yogi and the fakir. The other three ways require distancing oneself in one way or another from everyday life, whereas the fourth way takes place in life.

According to Peter Ouspensky, the minimum requirement for starting the fourth way work is to be a good householder, which means having a well-regulated life. It implies things like paying bills on time, looking after one's family and keeping one's friendships in good repair, simple but important things like that.

But what is a Way for? It starts from the pre-supposition that our usual level of consciousness is a kind of waking dream, and that it is possible to achieve higher, or one might say, clearer states of consciousness. The fourth way also provides practical tools to achieve this. Exercises which get in the way of our mechanical responses allow us to observe the habits and misunderstandings that obstruct clear consciousness.

The exercise of self-remembering, which is at the heart of the fourth way, is the effort to be aware of oneself at the same time as what one is looking at or sensing. This practice seems so obvious that we tend to imagine we are doing it anyway, until we actually try to do it. Then it becomes clear that most of the time we are identified with the thought or sensation of the moment, or some matter to do with the past or future. One's self is not in the picture, not in the now.

The effort of self-remembering if repeated often enough eventually strengthens in us, and we can learn to be present more often. We may become clearer that we are not that thought or feeling or object with which we are identified.

This state is very simple, even ordinary, and at the same time opens the question, who am I?

The second major exercise is the non-expression of negative emotions. From the point of view of ordinary psychology this presents a difficulty, because there appear to be only two alternatives: express frustration, anger and so on, or suppress it, and sometimes suppression can lead to pathological states. Suppressing anger, for example, can lead to depression, as anger is turned inwards on oneself as blame. A third way exists, however, which is to acknowledge the emotion in oneself without expressing it and without suppressing it either. This is a form of voluntary suffering. To succeed we have to be in a more objective state, that is, not identified. It is like saying to oneself, 'this too shall pass.' In this way we retain self-control and we retain the energy which would have been wasted had we 'let it all out.' This is very difficult and we can expect to fail more often than we succeed. The usefulness of this exercise, as with self-remembering, can only truly be verified by doing it.

The System as presented by George Gurdjieff, Peter Ouspensky and Rodney Collin comes with a great deal of other material, some of which may seem bizarre or at any rate not recognisable in terms of modern scientific understanding. However the fourth way also makes the request neither to believe nor to disbelieve any of the ideas presented. This is because, on the one hand the fourth way is intended to be a practical system rather than a belief system, and on the other hand in order to learn something new one must be prepared at least to entertain new ideas. It is important not to believe what one has not verified, but simply to hold these things in the mind as possibly true, possibly false, and possibly not correctly understood. A theory is not real until we have verified it.

If we believe too readily, the ideas themselves can become a kind of sleep. In the end only practice and personal verification count. Because of our human tendency to self-deception, verification has to be a continuous process, just as the effort to be present is.

SELF-REMEMBERING

Remember yourself always and everywhere.
—G. I. Gurdjieff

Remain attentive at every breath.
—Gudjduvani[17]

Self-remembering is at the centre of the System. In In search of the miraculous, Ouspensky quotes Gurdjieff as follows:

"Not one of you has noticed the most important thing that I have pointed out to you" he said. "That is to say, not one of you has noticed that you do not remember yourselves." (He gave particular emphasis to these words.) "You do not feel yourselves; you are not conscious of yourselves. With you, 'it observes' just as 'it speaks,' 'it thinks,' 'it laughs.' You do not feel: I observe, I notice, I see. Everything still 'is noticed,' 'is seen.' . . . In order really to observe oneself one must first of all remember oneself." (He again emphasized these words.) "Try to remember yourselves when you observe yourselves and later on tell me the results. Only those results will have any value that are accompanied by self-remembering. Otherwise you yourselves do not exist in your observations. In which case what are all your observations worth?"[18]

What is self-remembering? For me, it has mostly been the effort to be aware of myself as embodied in the present moment, but it is not impossible that I misunderstood the whole practice of self-remembering during my twenty-seven years in the school. So, here are some more indications from Ouspensky:

---

[17] Gudjduvani (12th century Sufi from Gudjduvan near Bokhara), cited in H. L. Shushud, The Masters of Wisdom of Central Asia, p.31

[18] In search of the miraculous, pp.117-8

So, at the same time as self-observing, we try to be aware of ourselves by holding the sensation of 'I am here'—nothing more.[19]

Q. When you say 'remember yourself,' do you mean by that to remember after you have observed yourself, or do you mean to remember the things we know are in us?

A. No, take it quite apart from observation. To remember oneself means the same thing as to be aware of oneself—'I am'. Sometimes it comes by itself; it is a very strange feeling. It is not a function, not thinking, not feeling; it is a different state of consciousness. By itself it only comes for very short moments, generally in quite new surroundings, and one says to oneself: 'How strange. I am here.' This is self-remembering; at this moment you remember yourself.[20]

Self-remembering is not really connected with memory; it is simply an expression. It means self-awareness or self-consciousness. One must be conscious of oneself.[21]

Self-remembering does not divide you, you must remember the whole, it is simply the feeling of 'I,' of your own person.[22]

Ouspensky vividly describes his first efforts at self-remembering in In Search of the Miraculous. He tries to be aware of himself while walking down the street, and succeeds until he reaches the tobacconist, and the next thing he remembers is 'waking up' in his flat.[23] He says that it is something that Western psychology has entirely missed, that we do not remember ourselves.

In what follows I describe self-remembering as I understood it as a member of the Fellowship. When I joined, it was considered to be the first principle of the fourth way.

---

[19] Fourth Way p.5

[20] ibid. p.8

[21] ibid. p.56

[22] ibid. p.107

[23] In Search of the Miraculous p.120

In his book *Self-Remembering* Robert Burton says that he speaks 'relentlessly about this dear old subject,' yet after the introduction of *the Sequence*, a short mantra to be recited inwardly, he barely spoke of it at all.[24]

From my own observation it seems to me that for almost all of my waking moments I was identified with one thing or another, and frequently drifted through life only minimally aware of my surroundings, beset by fears and imaginations. (This may or may not apply to you.) As Ouspensky points out, this very fact eludes us because if you ask someone, 'Are you awake?' then for that moment of course they are. We are not aware of our own *waking sleep*. In waking sleep (called in the System *second state*) thoughts move associatively just as they do in a sleeping dream (called in the System *first state*). The only difference is that real things intrude into our second state dream, putting an intermittent brake on the drift of associations.

To become properly aware of how much of our life is conducted in a dream, we have to make some effort to awaken. One method is self-remembering. This consists of the effort to be aware of the body at the same time as being aware of the object of one's attention, also known as divided attention. So one might be driving a car and be aware of the road ahead. That would usually be second state, attention in one direction. But then one could become aware of one's body in the driving seat and one's hands on the wheel at the same time. That would be divided attention, *self-remembering*. (The word *divided* is in a way misleading, because being aware of oneself at the same time as what one is observing is actually more complete, more whole, than one-directional attention.)

This seems almost banal until you actually try it. One loses the state very quickly. I once drove across London perfectly safely and when I got to my destination I realised I

---

[24] Robert Burton, *Self-Remembering*, p112

remembered nothing of the journey—that is the effect second state has—we remember very little. It is also commonplace to leave one's house and not remember locking the front door, so one has to go back to check (or worry about it all day). Once again, one was on auto-pilot and not present to one's surroundings.

As a new student I was advised by another student not to try to drive while practising self-remembering. The student thought this might be too distracting. Certainly when one first makes a deliberate effort of this kind there can be a tendency simply to move the focus of attention away from the road and onto one's bodily sensations, and of course that is not what is intended. One-pointed attention is ingrained. After some years of practice I no longer feel this is a problem. I am as prone to *waking sleep* as ever, but if I make the effort to self-remember then I can do it (and when driving I can be more attentive and almost certainly safer).

At first self-remembering can feel like a burdensome exercise, with presence coming only for a few seconds before one loses it again. But later it can appear almost (but not quite) without effort and sometimes can arise unexpectedly. As Ouspensky remarked, efforts of this kind are accompanied by a sense of peace.

I wrote 'one method' because there are others. In his book *On having no head*, Douglas Harding points out the apparently trivial fact that we do not experience ourselves as having a head. If I pay particular attention I can be aware of two sides of my nose on each side of my field of vision, but not my head. Nevertheless I go around imagining that I am what the mirror shows me, a person with a head. I carry around an image of myself that I do not experience (although of course other people will see that I have a head). To become aware of one's headlessness requires a similar effort to self-remembering, and carries with it a more intense awareness of one's surroundings.

These techniques have a lot in common with the now popular idea of mindfulness. The UK National Health Service web site states:

> Paying more attention to the present moment—to your own thoughts and feelings, and to the world around you—can improve your mental wellbeing.[25]

On the same page, Professor Mark Williams, former director of the Oxford Mindfulness Centre is quoted as saying:

> An important part of mindfulness is reconnecting with our bodies and the sensations they experience. This means waking up to the sights, sounds, smells and tastes of the present moment. That might be something as simple as the feel of a banister as we walk upstairs.

> Another important part of mindfulness is an awareness of our thoughts and feelings as they happen moment to moment.

> It's about allowing ourselves to see the present moment clearly. When we do that, it can positively change the way we see ourselves and our lives.

'Reconnecting with our bodies and the sensations they experience' sounds very like self-remembering. Efforts of this kind put one more closely in touch with what is actually happening, as opposed to the automatic internal monologue that passes for thought much of the time. One is no longer an imaginary picture of oneself walking through a largely imaginary world, sometimes tormented by unnecessary worries. Professor Williams again:

> This lets us stand back from our thoughts and start to see their patterns. Gradually, we can train ourselves to notice when our thoughts are taking over and realise that thoughts are simply 'mental events' that do not have to control us.

---

[25] www.nhs.uk/mental-health/self-help/tips-and-support/mindfulness/

Self-remembering does not remove suffering but it allows a different, more objective connection with it. It is possible to observe the suffering of one's body and emotions rather than being entirely absorbed in that suffering. The pain is no less, but at the same time something observes it impartially. This is not at all to harden the heart—on the contrary one feels emotional and physical pain just as much—but it does not rule one in the same way.

In the beginning it is easier to remember to make efforts to divide attention, to self-remember, when there is suffering. But there is equally a reward in self-remembering in happy circumstances. Whatever the situation, being present to each moment means that one is more intensely alive.

The present moment is for us the only real moment. The past is gone, represented by fragments of memory, like a threadbare cloth that after sufficient time barely hangs together, and we tend to fill the holes with what we think must have happened. The future is a theory or a dream. Only in the present moment can we do anything or experience anything.

Even so, when used in the context of belonging to a supposed school of awakening, there is room for self-deception, a feeling of peace that is in reality a subtle feeling of superiority, setting oneself apart from others, of smugness. 'I am awake among these sleeping beings.' Rather, the perception that for a particular moment you happen to be more awake, more in self-control than the person in front of you, should evoke compassion. *Noblesse oblige.* If you are more awake, you are more responsible. And your momentary superiority is not guaranteed for the next moment.

External consideration—considering the needs of others— requires an extra effort. I was once in a tranquil state sitting next to my wife, unaware that she was distressed by my seeming emotional remoteness. One of the problems of a cult is lack of attention to the needs of those not in the cult.

No real work worthy of the name should cut us off from our fellow mortals.

I have been asked, if self-remembering increases awareness, how is it that Robert Burton's students, who have supposedly devoted their lives to practising fourth way methods, end up believing a complex system of questionable ideas, arguably remote from reality?

The problem is not with self-remembering, nor with any other method of becoming more mindful and more grounded in the present. The problem is with a belief system in which the idea of ascending souls and multiple lifetimes takes one away from the present moment into a fantasy of immortality. It is possible to be aware in the present moment and still to have all manner of beliefs, and the state of presence has no immediate relation to whether the beliefs are true or not.

Paradoxically, the belief system of the fourth way is opposed to being here, now, because it is focussed on an imaginary future. Presenting self-remembering as a stepping stone to higher states immediately negates the value of simply being who one is, where one is.

A STATE OF HYPER-VIGILANCE

On a discussion forum an ex-student once criticised the whole idea of self-remembering. Why would one want to be in a constant state of hyper-vigilance?

A senior student once led a meeting in which he invited us to consider that he did not know how his foot got from flat on the floor to crossing his other leg, as though this were a problem, something to remark on. On reflection I am content to let my body do stuff without asking my permission every time, within reason.

To me, self-remembering is not a state of hyper-vigilance but a state in which one may rest in gentle alertness if one wishes to. Hyper-vigilance is more related to an adrenaline-fuelled state of 'fight-or-flight,' and I can quite see why trying to be in such a state would be uncomfortable.

There are clearly pitfalls in the fourth way work (known as the Work), opportunities for misunderstanding. This ought to be one of the reasons why the Work is carried out in schools, so that students can be mentored and misunderstandings corrected. The structure of the school I was in depended on the students teaching each other in meetings in the peripheral centres, and on big meetings led by Robert Burton in the headquarters. In practice everyone had their own path. I think the Teacher was detached from the students to a large extent, and the teaching was given as it were from on high rather than interactively. As time went on there were fewer and fewer and eventually no questions or observations from students in the big meetings. Put another way, the school such as it was, and in as far as it produced anything useful, was a product of its students working together with what we understood to be fourth way methods.

The misunderstanding in relation to self-remembering, though, would not be fully solved by discussion or mentoring within a fourth way school. This is because of the underlying assumption that persistent self-remembering will ultimately cause one to 'crystallise' as a higher being. Thus serious students of the fourth way try to practise self-remembering as often as possible, as a necessity, the failure at which will lead to their becoming food for the moon or lapsing into mere mechanical existence. In this way an exercise that can lead to being more at peace with oneself in the present moment, or what the Stoics called equanimity, instead becomes directed at a future and possibly imaginary accomplishment.

While in my experience practice makes coming into the present easier and more natural, it is open to question whether there is any merit in making it a moment-to-moment struggle. It is a tool, and how you use a tool depends on your aim.

EXERCISES AND FAILING AT EXERCISES

The School had various exercises which changed from time-to-time, designed to interrupt the automatic and mechanical functioning of the mind (or 'the machine' as it was referred to).

Once I started to follow the fourth way, for a long time I fought feelings of inadequacy and guilt that I could not remember myself consistently or do the prescribed exercises (like remembering to keep my feet flat on the floor while dining). After a while I realised that the exercises are merely tools—there is no merit or demerit in doing or failing to do the exercises. I was doing the work for myself, so other people's opinion didn't matter, and in any event, for the most part they couldn't see whether I was doing the work or not. Succeeding or failing is irrelevant: the point is to awaken in the moment.

In the words of the late, great physicist Richard Feynman, "What do you care what other people think?"

A further point, well made by others in the School, is that the moment you realise you have 'failed' in an exercise is a moment, albeit brief, of awakening. Progress is not always about success but about speed of recovery from failure.

For the guilt I do not blame the System but rather my own programming. Another saying of my early time in the School was: things as they are, myself as I am. Judgement of oneself and of others was not encouraged, so the System was not at fault in this.

For all the grievous faults and corruption in the heart of the Fellowship of Friends alleged elsewhere, it is possible for good advice to come from a bad source. To reject everything associated with a cult that one finally leaves is natural, but a mistake. Truth is truth no matter who says it, and good people can learn even from a bad teacher (but it's not an ideal way of spending time).

THE MYSTERY OF CONSCIOUSNESS

Consciousness is mysterious and occasions a lot of debate among scientists and philosophers, since on the one hand the prevailing scientific consensus is largely materialistic, and on the other there is no consensus as to how the flow of information in the brain can give rise to the sensation you have of being you.[26]

We can understand how to explain atoms in terms of hypothesised quarks, and chemistry in terms of atoms and quantum mechanics. Then we can begin to understand biochemistry in terms of chemistry and, on the next level up, the mechanisms of living cells in terms of biochemistry. But to try to explain cell biology in terms of quarks would be absurd. To explain the life of a complex animal in terms of atoms would also be absurd, since a whole new explanatory language is required at each level. Even so we accept that in principle there is a chain of relationships from life all the way down to the subatomic level. Whether we could in principle extend this chain of explanations upwards to consciousness is unresolved—or perhaps in trying to explain consciousness we are asking a question that is not properly put.

The purpose of this side discussion is to avoid making the assumption that because there are (or might be) 'higher' states of consciousness, it necessarily follows that, for example, panpsychism is true (the doctrine that everything is to some degree conscious, or alternatively that everything is ultimately made out of consciousness).

This is important because if 'higher' states of consciousness can be demonstrated it does not automatically give licence to all kinds of hand-waving woo, and on the other hand if we reject hand-waving woo it does not follow that we must reject the possibility of 'higher' states of consciousness.

---

[26] Dennett, Daniel C., *Consciousness explained*, Penguin 1993, p.22

As I see it, the existence of a higher state of consciousness would probably not make a lot of difference to the arguments between materialists and those who believe that ordinary consciousness is something special and non-material.

STATES OF CONSCIOUSNESS: FIRST, SECOND AND THIRD STATE

'Higher' states of consciousness were regularly explained and demonstrated (up to a point) in the introductory meetings I attended, and occasionally led, at the London branch of our fourth way school.

Up to now I have put 'higher' in inverted commas because it is a commonplace that altered states can be produced, for example with alcohol, without there being anything 'higher' about them (other than being pleasant). The desire in humans for altered states is almost universal. Some cultures that ban alcohol permit tobacco and coffee, for example. Children sometimes play the game of spinning round until they feel dizzy, or the trick of squatting, nose-holding against expiration (Valsalva) and then suddenly standing up, to produce a momentary pre-faint. In the '60s hallucinogens were popular with some groups of people.

According to the fourth way, at any rate as I was taught it, some drugs can give you a taste of higher states but these states are not permanent, they do not belong to you and are not under your control. Thus, on meeting the fourth way it is necessary to give up the use of drugs for this purpose.

The explanation of different levels of consciousness as we gave it in the introductory meetings is as follows:[27]

The first level (first state) is sleep. We did not distinguish between dreaming and dreamless sleep.

Second state is 'waking sleep' and is what we call normal waking consciousness, but according to the fourth way this is little different from first state. In second state most of our thought, behaviour and speech is automatic, a kind of word-

---

[27] See also Psychology p.20

association, or like a pinball machine, in which one thing follows another associatively. 'Man is a machine' according to Gurdjieff. That this is the usual state of the mind is readily observable by anyone willing to be an objectively impartial observer. At any rate, I'll bet I'm not the only one to have a mind that very often runs all by itself to very little purpose. The process can also be observed in normal non-academic conversation. Where a conversation begins and where it ends are usually unrelated.

Third state is self-remembering. Everything else is still going on, but we can make a little effort to be simultaneously aware of our own bodies. It is not just stuff going on, but ourselves as part of what is going on. One might say, we are actors in what is taking place. It is a subtle but at the same time a major shift in perspective. One jumps in and out of it suddenly, like that optical illusion which is now a rabbit, now a duck.

We used to induce this state by asking attendees at the meeting simply to fall silent and become aware of the weight of the body on the chair, the air on the face, the flowers in the vase, the sounds coming into the room from outside.

THE THIRD STATE, SELF-REMEMBERING AND MINDFULNESS

In my experience it is the case that third state exists and is accessible to anyone who wants it. It is also my experience that the ability to enter the third state improves with practice. The use of it is to be able to step back a little way from situations in which one finds oneself immersed (or better, entangled—in the term Ouspensky used, identified), to gain a little objectivity.

Third state does not abolish real pain. However it puts one into a different relation to it. The experience of discomfort at the dentist does not go away through self-remembering, but somehow the acceptance of the pain puts one a little more in control of one's feelings about it. Just the pain without the imagination. This also applies to inner emotional pain: one acknowledges it rather than trying unsuccessfully to pretend it isn't there or struggling with it like Brer Rabbit and the Tar Baby.

Third state is also a place of peace, as mentioned by Peter Ouspensky.[28]

Some in the school used to make a distinction between self-remembering and third state, to the effect that self-remembering is the effort required to get to the third state. In my understanding the two are the same, although it is also true that in the beginning one tries very hard to remember oneself and usually passes most of the day forgetting, and after some years of practice one can slip into third state relatively easily. It works best if you don't try too hard. But you have to try too hard to get to the point where you realise that trying too hard stands in the way of simply resting in the state. (It is similar to the paradox that if you want to attract a member of the opposite sex—or same sex—trying too hard will cause them to run away, and if you don't try at all, nothing happens.)

Is third state similar to mindfulness? I would say, probably yes. I don't know much about the mindfulness movement but I was once talked through a mindfulness exercise called 'body scan' or something like that. It consisted of lying flat on the floor and gradually becoming aware of the sensations of the body, starting from the feet and working upwards. That is one way of coming into the present moment and letting the preoccupations of the moment drop away. Self-remembering might be described as a form of walking meditation to reach that calm state among the ordinary activities of everyday life.

---

[28] In Search of the Miraculous p.120

YOU ARE NOT YOUR THOUGHTS

And after the earthquake a fire; but the Lord was not in the fire: and after the fire a still small voice.
—1 Kings 19:12

You are not your thoughts. Anything that can be observed is not the observer.

Ouspensky wrote somewhere that we are not responsible for what we think, only for what we do. It is possible to have fears or fantasies that we might do this or that which we ourselves recognise as cruel or criminal, or self-accusatory thoughts which come into our minds unbidden and unwanted. How can we work with such thoughts?

Anyone who has had recurrent unwanted thoughts or urges will have found that trying to get rid of them simply makes them stronger. It is near-impossible to stop thoughts by an act of will: it is like the instruction to stop thinking of elephants. Even the apparently simple exercise of trying to stop thoughts for one minute is almost bound to fail.

There is indeed a place of peace when unnecessary thoughts settle like dust after the rain. You have to go about it some other way. Better to accept them, as though watching interesting fish in a pond. There is no need to jump into the pond or to feed the fish if you don't want to.

There is no need to struggle with unwanted thoughts and no need to give them the energy of undue attention. 'I have seen you before,' is one possible inner response. The same old stuff goes around again and again. We must of course not act on thoughts and urges that may be harmful, and if that is a struggle, so be it. But being in that quiet place of the observer gives us a much stronger place to work from than being in the thoughts themselves. Let it be, and do nothing. This is also voluntary suffering.

MANTRAS

The effect of chanting a mantra, internally or aloud, is to displace thought. Mantras are not a feature of the fourth way as I understand it, but the silent expression of work 'I's, short sentences or words whose aim is to help awakening, is intended at least to replace useless thoughts with useful ones.

In the Fellowship, Robert Burton invented something called 'the Sequence' which was or is a string of six single-syllable work 'I's strung together and works much like a short mantra. While I found it moderately useful some of the time, it would get in the way of being simply present, and its main use was to abandon it once one was in the moment. Doing exercises is not an end in itself, but being present to one's life is. In the fourth way the central and original technique for freeing the mind from useless associations is self-remembering.

In the SES a sitting mantra meditation was used, which one does for twenty minutes twice a day. It is the transcendental meditation introduced by Maharishi Mahesh Yogi and it was taught to SES students, when I was a member, by the Study Society, an organisation founded by Ouspensky's student Dr Francis Roles. Initiation in those days cost a week's pay, and since I was a student on a grant at the time, this did not amount to very much money in absolute terms. I was told that the mantra given was personal to me, however it became apparent later that everyone in the SES youth group had been given the same mantra.

INNER CONSIDERING AND EXTERNAL CONSIDERING

I remember, fairly early on in my membership of the Fellowship, freeing myself just a little from a state of psychological imprisonment.

In those days some meetings were held in a rented room above some shops in Cricklewood Broadway, North London. We were sitting in a circle in a rather plain room with grey wall-to-wall carpet. I remember the carpet because I was staring at it, not feeling able to make eye contact with anyone. Something that I had learned or absorbed made me realise that there was nothing to fear. I don't remember exactly what freed me from the fear of looking up. Perhaps I understood, as I did later, that no-one was judging me, or if they were then it was not my problem.

The idea that someone is judging us is called in Ouspensky's terminology, *inner considering*.

Inner considering, that is, worrying about what other people think, or even what they might have thought as a result of some incident long ago and that they have since long forgotten, used to haunt me. It still does occasionally, and I find myself saying some word out loud in connection with some memory of something which illustrates just what a socially-inept idiot I was (or imagine myself to have been) back then. This of course is an absurd way to spend any waking moments which might otherwise be employed in just observing the world go by and responding to it appropriately. Ouspensky draws attention to this waste of energy in connection with identification in general.[29]

One cure for it is self-remembering, plus the thought that no-one is thinking much about you because if they're thinking about you at all they're thinking about what you are thinking about them.

External considering is quite the opposite of inner considering, and is sometimes said to be the emotional aspect of self-remembering. It is being attentive to the needs of others.

All kinds of subjective considerations can get in the way, such as doing or not doing what other people expect, or considerations of one's own benefit, or assuaging guilt, or wanting acceptance. Self-remembering is a way of being aware of the needs of the present moment in a clean state of

---

[29] In Search of the Miraculous p.191

mind. Being aware of oneself as an actor makes it easier to step aside from one's various identifications.

Again I am struck by something discordant about the Fellowship. Once I described to a visiting senior student an episode that had happened to me while queuing in a bank. I had noticed an old woman who was obviously having some difficulty standing in the queue, which was moving slowly. Inner considering held me back from offering her my place, because that meant breaking out of my shyness and attracting attention. In the end I did. I intended this as an illustration of the power of going against programming. However the senior student reacted quite forcefully that this was not the way. To the best of my understanding she objected to what she imagined was quite the opposite: me acting out of a mechanical sense of duty or obligation, feminine dominance (see later). I kept my counsel and did not defend myself, feeling that this was a misunderstanding. However the view that students should act against mechanical goodness on principle seemed to me at the time and seems to me now as illogical. If one would mechanically and automatically do the right thing, then do it, otherwise one is attempting what Gurdjieff said is impossible, conscious evil. Being conscious of your mechanical actions does not necessarily mean you should do something different.

Let me state that more clearly. Refraining from doing the right thing because someone else might think it is mechanical, is stupid.

IDENTIFICATION

We tend to get absorbed into things—ideas, beliefs, feelings of personal injustice, why that person pushed into the queue while I was waiting in the sandwich shop, that the newspaper edited out the crucial sentence in my letter to the editor and made it worse by committing an apostrophe error, and so on. I am enjoying the cake so much I practically become the cake.

In order not to be swept along by events in this way a little objectivity is required. I am not a ball in a pin-ball machine. Avoiding identification, or at least being able to jump out of the system when finding oneself in a pin-ball machine, is about being a full human being. We don't need to get involved in the idea of trying to be higher beings in order to see the sense of this.

THE NON-EXPRESSION OF NEGATIVE EMOTIONS

Resentment is like taking poison and waiting for the other fellow to die.
—Anon.

But I say unto you, Love your enemies, bless them that curse you, do good to them that hate you, and pray for them which despitefully use you, and persecute you.
—Matthew 5:44

One of the first exercises we were given in the SES was not to criticise. This seems odd when criticism is so normal in everyday life, and indeed constructive criticism is often essential. We even sometimes ask for it, then summon up the courage to listen in silence and take it, if we are strong enough. It is one way (mercifully not the only way) to learn and grow.

What I think was meant by the exercise was rather to eschew criticism in the sense of mere negative commentary. There is a big difference, for example, between saying, "That child will never be a dancer because she's too fat," (a comment heard in relation to a girl rehearsing for an end of term performance) and what could reasonably have been said instead: "Look at her enthusiasm! She'll make it some day if she carries on like that!" We often criticise out of ignorance, or we fail to see the positive for a perceived imperfection. We also tend to have internal negative commentary about ourselves, unless we're so trapped and desperate that we buffer it with false pride. Internal criticism turns into depression; directed outwards it turns to anger or cynicism.

An exercise related to not criticising, in the fourth way as taught by Ouspensky, is the non-expression of negative emotions.

Not expressing negative emotions is not the same as repressing them, but it does mean observing them and resisting the temptation to express them, which because of ingrained habits is very hard. It is quite possible to hold one's ground if necessary and state calmly but firmly what is and is not acceptable, and in most situations this is actually a successful strategy. Becoming angry usually results in a similar reaction from the other person, with both becoming entrenched in a particular position irrespective of the rights and wrongs of the case. Both compromise and understanding become impossible.

Sometimes we find ourselves in a situation in which we feel we have been wronged and we want it put right. We want the shopkeeper to give a refund for something that is not satisfactory, and we are indignant about it. The shopkeeper responds with intransigence on the ground that we don't have the receipt. We get a little angry and raise our voice. The shopkeeper responds by folding her arms, or calls the manager who comes out with a stony face and a fixed attitude. Now let's roll back the time to when we entered the shop. "I have a problem I hope you can help me with." This is an entirely different dynamic, and puts the shopkeeper immediately in the mood to be helpful and to bend any rules that fall into a grey area.

Having control of my temper puts me in control of myself, and losing control of my temper often means losing control both of myself and of the situation. In practical terms this is not dissimilar to the technique of assertiveness training, in which one calmly asserts what is and is not acceptable. What is my aim? Do I want to express negativity or do I want things to turn out how I want them to?

In relation to someone I have had issues with in the past, I find it useful to approach a new encounter with that person as though the past were wiped clean. Of course I will be cautious: the principle of 'once bitten, twice shy' applies, and this is not an invitation to naivety. Nevertheless, starting afresh gives the other person the opportunity to behave differently, freed from my and their preconceptions from previous times. If they don't take the opportunity, nothing much is lost.

There may be circumstances, particularly during a process of healing, in which it is necessary and useful to let feelings of anger out. This, I suggest, would usually be in the context of acknowledging the feelings, and much less often in expressing them to the person who occasioned them in the first place. However it is wise to avoid absolute statements—there are likely to be exceptions.

So far what I have written is no different from advice available from any number of non-esoteric sources. However according to Ouspensky the expression of negative emotions drains energy that could be used for creating consciousness, or in Gurdjieff's term, creating a soul. This relates to the idea of higher hydrogens, the first and second conscious shocks and the food diagram (of which more later).

VOLUNTARY SUFFERING AND UNNECESSARY SUFFERING

Voluntary suffering does not mean wearing a hair shirt or self-flagellation. It means not kicking against the goads.[30]

Things are what they are. What we wish to change we can try to change. What we can't change we must learn to accept. But to complain about what we can't change is just a waste of energy, and creates additional turmoil inside us which is rightly called unnecessary suffering.

Complaining is a negative emotion, resentment is another. In modern parlance it is 'could-have, would-have, should-

---

[30] Acts 9:5

have.' It is weakness. If you could have but didn't, let it go. Start from where you are. The present moment dissolves the idiocies of the past, not so as to repair them, but so as to avoid repeating them.

Always consider your aim—what do you want to happen? What will happen if you express what you feel—will things be better or worse? Will it matter a year from now? Ouspensky claimed that there is nothing noble, beautiful or strong in negative emotions.[31]

There is a nobility and strength in swallowing suffering. If you must complain at all, complain once only. The Stoics see this as part of equanimity. Despite the suffering, it is a place of calm and inward confidence.

It is perhaps easier to bear difficulty if we believe that somehow by doing so it will help our spiritual awakening. But if we let drop away the unproven apparatus of belief we can see that it makes sense not to have unnecessary suffering right now. Ouspensky was asked what you get for giving up your unnecessary suffering. He replied, "the absence of [unnecessary] suffering."[32]

True and false personality

According to the System we are born without personality, which the Fellowship calls *false personality*. As babies we are in *essence*: intelligent but guileless.[33] Personality is a mask through which we deal with the world and behind which we hide.[34]

In Grimm's fairytale of that name, *Maid Maleen* refuses to marry the man her father the king has chosen for her.[35]

---

[31] Psychology p.71

[32] Fourth Way p.373

[33] In Search of the Miraculous pp.160-165, The Fourth Way pp.79-83.

[34] Personality: Latin persona, a mask, as worn by an actor. Skeat, An Etymological Dictionary of the English Language.

[35] Manheim (translator), Grimm's Tales, Gollancz 1993, pp.606-610

Instead she is in love with the true prince. To prevent this marriage the king locks Maid Maleen and her maidservant in a stone tower with sufficient food for seven years. The true prince rides past and calls her name, but she cannot hear him because of the thickness of the walls.

In the terms of the fourth way system, Maid Maleen could be seen as essence seeking the fulfilment of her full potential, represented by the prince. The stone tower represents the protection from the outside world by personality that essence hides behind.

A catastrophic war follows in which the kingdom is laid waste apart from the tower itself. What prompts Maid Maleen to try to escape from the tower is that no-one comes to rescue her at the end of the seven years and the food is running out. Using the bread knife she and her servant finally work one of the stones loose and escape. If we are unable to take this step then we must starve in personality and essence will die. We become something that in the beginning we were not.

That is not the end of the story, and Maid Maleen must eat nettles, use deception and risk death in order to come to her true stature as a princess.

In The Great Divorce C. S. Lewis describes a fictional tragic struggle between essence and personality in which personality wins. But personality is a construct, an act. In Lewis's story, having defeated essence the personality disappears—there is nothing real left.[36]

In the Fellowship we also had the concept of true personality. We were told that true personality is the result of school work, and enables us to function in the world and at the same time protect essence without false personality taking over. In The Fourth Way Ouspensky refers to useful parts of personality, parts that can support the work of

---

[36] C. S. Lewis, The Great Divorce, Fount Harper Collins 1997, pp.91-100

awakening, but he does not call this 'true personality.' I have not found it called this in any of the fourth way books.

I believe that the distinction between essence and personality is useful. Sometimes we come across people so trapped in their imaginary picture of themselves, in the character they are acting, that it is difficult to find the real person behind the mask. For all of us, once we begin to trust someone and get to know them we begin cautiously to drop our mask, to become more ourselves. Even if we have to act through personality, it is possible to abstain from believing in the act. We may well have to use such acts, especially in difficult and challenging situations, but I have found that authenticity is usually a workable strategy. Seeing the gap between the person I should like others to believe I am and the truth frees me to be who I am. It is also what enables me, when appropriate, to apologise.

Is true personality only the result of school work? I doubt it. I think what it refers to is honesty, authenticity, and the courage to be ourselves.

How do we get there? I think by letting go of self-importance yet being confident that we are valuable as we are.

INSIDE THE FELLOWSHIP

MEETINGS

Every thing possible to be believ'd is an image of truth.
—William Blake[37]

In my early days in the Fellowship there were up to twenty members in the London Centre, and new students came and went fairly often. I attended meetings about once a week, which were held in what was called 'The Teaching House,' a rented house in a pleasant suburb of London. The rent was partly paid by students who lived there and partly by contributions from other London members.

We sat around the room usually in a circle and there would be a vase of flowers placed in the centre of the room. Someone would lead the meeting, usually supported by another student who might or might not say anything. There would be a Work topic, and meeting leaders had a free choice as to what they would talk about, although it was always about something in the fourth way as understood in the Fellowship.

Often the topic would have been announced the week before so that students could make personal observations prior to the meeting in relation to some exercise or other than had been proposed. It might be, for example, some simple way of 'interrupting sleep' such as not saying 'you know.' Of course I would often forget. This, it was said, was the opportunity to awaken in that moment.

One's observations would be presented as an *angle*. The idea of an angle is to get away from the idea that there is only one right point of view. Except for deliberate lies or misunderstandings of fact, every point of view is correct: it is just that each of us looks at a question from a different angle. Even so, someone's genuine observation could easily evoke

---

[37] *The Marriage of Heaven and Hell*

someone else's *opposite* 'I's, the tendency we all have to see what is wrong with what another person is saying instead of trying to understand. Often disputes are merely about the imprecise use of words, or inferring some meaning that has not been intended. Sometimes what appear to be two opposite points of view are actually capable of both being true at the same time. School exercises at the time included substituting 'and' for 'but' and not giving opposite 'I's. Although logic was not mentioned, in fact this is usually perfectly consistent with formal logic. The contrary of 'A' is not 'B,' it is simply 'not-A.'

At first I had to curb my own tendency to want to speak, as though my opinions were in a pressure cooker. In such a state it was difficult or impossible for me properly to understand what others were saying, and my opinion, expressed or not, remained unchanged and I learned nothing. I understood, though, that the London Centre was a place inimical to *false personality*, what one might call 'ego.' Once I let go of that I was able more often to rest in a state of essence.

It was also a relief to me not to have to feel that I must make small-talk, and it was fine to remain silent. I still find that making small-talk requires effort, but it is part of what the Work calls *external consideration*, that is, considering the needs of others, and is therefore necessary sometimes. But in the Fellowship you can be silent and no-one feels uncomfortable because of this, as long as you acknowledge their presence. Words are sometimes a barrier to communication.

Something I remember from early meetings is the idea of *creating memory*. Someone would occasionally do something unexpected to *create a state*. Once for example, during a moment of silence, a student cut off a rosebud from the flower arrangement and ate it. Years later the idea of creating memory in this sort of way seemed to have been forgotten. I think we became a little stale, less experimental.

CENTRE DINNERS

A practice regularly observed in my early days in the London Centre, but later fallen into disuse, was the Centre Dinner (dinners with the Teacher, however, continue in Apollo). One could participate as a server or as a guest. My first experience was as a guest. The idea was to create a fine dining experience. There would be a freshly ironed linen table cloth and a small centrepiece of flowers.

The guests would be greeted at the door and their coats hung up, and then ushered into the living room where pre-dinner drinks would be served. Meanwhile other students would be working with food preparation, serving and 'restoration' (clearing up).

Once the guests were seated and before the start of dinner one of the serving students or one of the diners would read a poem or other inspiring text.

Everything would be done very intentionally. Courses were served to the left of each diner and empty plates taken from the right. I do not know if this is normal in high-end dining but it was supposed to symbolise giving to essence and taking away from false personality.

There would be one diner whose job it was to guide conversation. There would usually be a chosen topic, or it might flow from the poem. Diners would raise a hand if they wished to give an 'angle' and the designated leader would indicate who should speak.

In this way conversation was kept to a high level and on topic. While to someone not used to it this might sound tedious, in fact it allowed the mind to rest.

The aim of events like these was to encourage presence, and this was achieved partly by what was called *intentionality* or using the *kings of centres*, which is explained later.

IMPRESSIONS OF RENAISSANCE

I first travelled to Apollo, then called Renaissance, within a year of joining the Fellowship. The property is a large area of hills and a few small lakes in a remote part of northern California. To get there the only way is by car, and it takes about six hours. I hired a car from San Francisco airport and used a map supplied by the car rental company combined with sketched instructions from one of the London Centre Directors. In those days there was no sat-nav. I passed over the Oakland bridge, on through low hills and then a long journey in the flat rather drab landscape which is mostly farming and vineyards. Then the landscape changed to the foothills of the Sierra Nevada, climbing up through hills laced with conifers and scrub, eventually passing Collins Lake shortly to reach the small town of Oregon House, then off the main highway towards the property.

In those days it was traditional that Fellowship students from around the world would travel to Renaissance in September for the grape harvest. The hills on the property had almost all been terraced to grow grape vines and the Renaissance winery had become known for producing some very high quality wines in small volumes.

Nothing was compulsory, but there was little point in being there unless you joined in. We were given rubber gloves and secateurs and shown how to gather the bunches of grapes. A small tractor with a trailer ran between the rows for us to empty the grapes into.

Simple but delicious food was provided for lunch. One had to book for the evening meal. Both meals were provided in a building on top of a hill with beautiful views over the property, including a terrace when the weather was fine, which it usually was. This was originally called 'The Lodge' but was renamed 'Apollo d'Oro' ('Golden Apollo') later on, when the property began to be decorated with large baroque statues which Robert Burton had had gilded.

In spite of my natural shyness I found it easy to introduce myself and join conversations. The other students were gentle and none were loud or overbearing—I attribute this to the exercises of not expressing negative emotions and of putting false personality in abeyance. Whether in any individual the gentleness was yet another act of personality or was genuine I could not tell—I felt it was genuine. In any case there is a saying in ordinary life, 'fake it till you make it.' Either way it was safe to be in essence, unguarded. If by chance anyone did express negativity towards me, that was their problem not mine.

The topic of conversation was almost always 'the Work.' This was hardly surprising given that students were from many different backgrounds and from many parts of the world. 'The Work' was the school equivalent of talking about the weather.

Most days during harvest there were meetings led by the teacher, Robert Burton. Originally students would give *angles* related to the topic. In subsequent years the meetings would become more and more controlled, with angles being pre-printed on cards—some of the angles would be from students, submitted in advance, but mostly they were one-liners from 'conscious beings'—Jesus, Buddha, Lao Tzu, or others of the forty-four designated by Robert. If a student thought the angle they had been given was relevant they would raise their hand and stand to read the angle if called upon. In later years this became even more controlled, and Robert's helpers would read angles which would be projected onto large television screens together with related images.

Over the years I made several trips to Apollo, and at each visit the beautiful impressions increased: a fountain featuring a large statue of Poseidon surrounded by ornamental fishes that spouted water in a circle, tall pencil-thin cypresses near the border of the property and leading up to the winery, rows of cycads along the road leading up to Apollo d'Oro, roundabouts at the road intersections later adorned with flags and gilded statues on pedestals, and a rose garden with pergolas.

The most impressive building was, on my first visit, the Ming Museum, which at that time housed probably the finest collection of Ming dynasty furniture in the world. The museum from the outside was quite a good pastiche of a single-storey French chateau, and inside it was austere and minimalist, with polished wood floors. In the early days Robert encouraged this minimalist style, and there was a joke that on a night out students would paint the town beige.

On later trips the Ming furniture was gone, sold, and Robert had moved back into what had been the museum, which now became his personal dwelling, apart from the main hall in the centre which was used for meetings. The museum, later re-named the Academy, gradually became filled with antiques inspired by Robert Burton's visits to the Musée Jaquemart-André in Paris and the Wallace Collection in London. The central hall had Louis XIV-style furniture upholstered in pink moire fabric, with similar fabric in panels on the walls which were also adorned with paintings by a Fellowship student G., of Egyptian gods and floral decorations. In front of a huge mirror were candle-holders and clocks supported by gilded nude figures. There was a large golden angel flying above an antique French tapestry. This hung behind the area where Robert Burton would sit for meetings, raised on a dais and flanked with whichever students were chosen for this honour. On another wall was the painting *The Toilet of Venus* by Guercino (the painting was the subject of a dispute with the Italian government, I understand).

The entrance lobby after the double front doors and before the meeting hall later had a ceiling painting, also by G., which included a naked Venus in a double scallop shell and a naked flying man with a full-on erection. The quality of the work was of a very high order and so somehow did not seem obscene, although I'm not sure I'd want it in a public space.

To the front and the back of the Academy was a rose garden, and to one side a potager, a vegetable garden arranged in a semi-circle and decorated with occasional French statues in the classical manner, of goddesses and cherubs. It was unquestionably a beautiful place to be in. On the other side another garden in a more intimate style was made, including a small covered area devoted to bonsai trees.

As Apollo developed, other features were added: large marquees in an Indian style for outdoor meetings, an Indian wooden screen and a large dancing Shiva.

The winery did not flourish financially, despite the quality of its wines. One of the winemakers left the school and continues to produce small batches of wine nearby. Most of the vine terraces are now neglected. The school is supported largely or solely from the contributions of students (I assume: no-one outside the central elite ever sees the account books).

One major source of income was clearly the events for which students from around the world would visit. One gave one's time for free, and volunteering was genuinely voluntary. But the events themselves were expensive. That one had paid one's dues did not entitle one to attend even a meeting with the Teacher without additional payment. Teaching dinners were expensive. One could (entirely voluntarily) have one's picture taken with Robert, or split the cost between several students. I used to have many of these photographs. Distaste for what I have come to understand about Robert has led to my destroying them.

UNDER A STARRY SKY

I remember particularly my last-but-one visit to Apollo. It was late summer. My days were spent volunteering: sometimes in the kitchen but more often moving chairs and tables for outdoor events in sometimes sweltering heat. I would also attend Robert's events, not only meetings but also dining events.

For all of Robert's events one would dress formally. There would be teaching breakfasts and teaching dinners at which smaller numbers of students were served excellent food by other students while listening to Robert talk. Relatively little food actually got eaten because it was understood that one did not eat while someone else was talking. Robert would do most of the talking, supplemented by occasional contributions from students when we felt called upon.

Somehow a magical atmosphere of peace was created from the moment one arrived. A student would be handing out glasses either of sparkling wine or orange juice depending on one's choice, and one would wait under the palm trees, talking softly. It was possible also to wait in silence without embarrassment or tension. Everyone smiled. I never felt I had to smile, it just happened that way.

There was a very large outdoor dining event one evening. During the day I had been part of a large team of students from around the world setting out chairs and tables, fitting lamps in trees, and placing table cloths, cutlery and table decorations. I had time to go back to where I was staying, change into a dinner suit and return as a guest. It seemed that every visitor was there, one way or another. It was not long before the sun set and the night sky, free of light pollution, showed the Milky Way arcing across pure black. The air was warm and comforting. There was a very good mariachi band composed also of fellow students. Before any food was brought out a number of songs were played, with musician M. introducing each song with a translation in English from the original Spanish. These translations, delivered in M's calm English accent, were amusingly quirky, as translations from a passionate culture into an English-speaking one can tend to be.

At each small table were some who knew each other and some who did not. Conversation was easy and not memorable, faces lit by candle-light and the light from the lamps in the trees. This atmosphere of gentle joy was what the school was particularly good at.

My last visit to Apollo was with my new wife, who was also a member at that time, but was new to the school. Robert sent a student to check her out and presumably report back.

The student was very sweet, but I never understood the purpose of that encounter. It may be of relevance that over the years I had been a consistent and significant contributor in terms of membership payments. I think I was important, but not very important.

A DOORWAY TO THE FANTASTIC

The fourth way is not an invention of Robert Earl Burton, although Robert Earl Burton's version is.

The fourth way emerged from the teaching of George Gurdjieff, an Armenian Greek, brought up in the cathedral city of Kars in what is now eastern Turkey. Gurdjieff, according to his own account, gathered around him a small group of seekers of wisdom, and came back from Central Asia with the System.

Gurdjieff taught his version of the System in Russia where he was joined by Russian writer and thinker Peter Ouspensky. Whereas Ouspensky was an intellectual, Gurdjieff was rather an unashamed trickster (read for example The Material Question in Gurdjieff's Meetings with Remarkable Men).[38] Gurdjieff claimed that he had learned the System from a mysterious monastery in Central Asia, the Sarmoung Brotherhood, which has never been identified. He presented what he had learned in a bizarre nomenclature that was probably of his own devising, in which there are traces of Greek and probably other languages (for example, what Ouspensky later called the Law of Seven Gurdjieff calls Heptaparaparshinokh). Ouspensky unpicked the language, systematised it and re-presented the System in terms that at least appear clear.

Ouspensky eventually parted company with Gurdjieff for reasons that are differently stated in different sources, but which amount to Ouspensky feeling that the direction of Gurdjieff's work had changed, in particular that whereas Gurdjieff had initially insisted on personal verification, he later seemed to be requiring his students to take everything

---

[38] G. I. Gurdjieff, Meetings with Remarkable Men, Penguin Arkana 1985 pp.247ff

on trust.[39] The tension between personal verification and unexamined belief is a theme that I shall return to from time-to-time in this essay.

All the successors of Gurdjieff as far as I know went in search of Influence C. According to Ouspensky, *Influence C*, otherwise known as 'conscious influence,' is the direct communication of esoteric truth from someone who has previously received it.[40] Ouspensky felt that the System was incomplete (*In Search of the Miraculous* was originally entitled *Fragments of an Unknown Teaching*) and in particular that it lacked a simple method for students to become conscious. He experimented, for example, with continuous prayer.[41]

Student of Gurdjieff, J. G. Bennett describes part of his search for a teacher in *Journeys in Islamic Lands*, and Ouspensky's student Rodney Collin travelled to Mexico looking for inspiration among the pyramids of Oaxaca.[42] Dr Francis Roles, the student of Ouspensky who continued the Ouspensky Work in London and founded the Study Society, and Leon MacLaren who founded the School of Economic Science (SES), eventually met the Maharishi. From the Maharishi they learned the meditation method known as Transcendental Meditation, but resisted the Maharishi's attempts to take over their organisations. Instead they went to the source, the Maharishi's teacher, the Shankaracharya. In this way the SES and the Study Society claim the continuation and development of the fourth way System through the connection with the Advaita philosophy of India.[43] Gerald de Symons Beckwith of the Study Society says that the knowledge of liberation manifests in different guises

---

[39] Ouspensky, *A Record of Meetings*, entry for 9 October 1935

[40] *Psychology* p.57

[41] Beckwith, *Ouspensky's Fourth Way*, p.242

[42] J.G.Bennett, *Journeys in Islamic Lands*; Joyce Collin-Smith, *Call No Man Master*

[43] Beckwith pp.73-80

at different times and places, and indeed the intention to adapt the System to the Western mind was explicit in Gurdjieff's activities from the beginning. The SES, of which I was a member for four years, had adopted Vedantic Sanskrit terminology by the time I was a member, and the Study Society mixes the Vedanta with Ouspensky's terminology.[44]

The origin of Gurdjieff's branch of the System itself could be from the Sufis of Central Asia. J. G. Bennett in his joint work with H. L. Shushud, *Masters of Wisdom of Central Asia* (based on translations of medieval texts), attributes to Gudjduvani the idea of self-remembering in a very similar phrase to that used by Gurdjieff—'Remember yourself always and in all situations.'[45] However this phrase does not appear in the version authored by Shushud alone.[46]

If you look on Google Maps and drop the little yellow man onto a photograph in, say Samarkand or Khorezm, you will see dusty towns with the usual drab twentieth century commercial buildings and flats, and scattered around, extraordinary mosques the size of cathedrals or small forts, decorated in exquisite coloured tiles. These speak to the existence in the past of something remarkable, just as we stand in awe of the medieval cathedrals of Europe.

INFLUENCE C IN THE FELLOWSHIP

When I joined the Fellowship I never questioned its authenticity as a fourth way school. I simply accepted the rules, did the exercises and enjoyed the sense of being on a meaningful journey. I felt I was able to verify the teacher through the people around me and the teaching itself. At no point did the question of lineage arise as a problem for me.

---

[44] ibid.

[45] Shushud and Bennett, *The masters of wisdom of Central Asia*, Systematics vol. 6, no. 4, March 1969, p.4

[46] "Remain attentive with every breath," in Shushud, *Masters of Wisdom of Central Asia*, p.31

Once I was asked about it in a prospective student meeting and replied that the System came to our teacher through Rodney Collin and Alex Horn, Robert Burton's teacher. After the meeting another student quite rightly said to me that we shouldn't claim a connection with Rodney Collin because we don't know this for certain.

Lineage was always claimed by Robert Burton through Alex Horn, but it is not at all clear what connection Horn had with the fourth way of Gurdjieff and Ouspensky. There is a suggestion that Horn visited Collin in Mexico, but there is scant evidence that he stayed for any length of time or learned anything from him. However according to Burton he, Burton, made direct contact with Influence C, understood as the disembodied spirits of previous conscious beings. He compiled a list of forty-four who are said to be guiding the school. According to Burton, Leonardo da Vinci whispers in his ear. He also claims that Influence C works directly with students.

In my early years in the Fellowship people would ask, "Have you verified Influence C?" At that time it was acceptable to admit that one hadn't. Verification consisted in co-incidences, what Jungians might call synchronicity. So one might on a poster or in a book see a quotation from one of the forty-four conscious beings identified by Robert Burton, and the quotation happened to answer a question that had been bothering one. This might occur on a few occasions and eventually one would take this as verification. In addition we were all sensitised to the number forty-four and in consequence saw the number forty-four everywhere.

Part of me was well aware of the tendency of the human mind to see patterns where there are none. But the idea of augury goes back a long way in human history. "There is special providence in the fall of a sparrow," as Shakespeare put it. The idea of Influence C as promoted by Robert Burton slipped into my belief system without much of a struggle, I am embarrassed to admit.

THE FOURTH WAY TO WHAT?

If I were to formulate from today's understanding what my aim was when I first joined SES at the age of seventeen, it would be to acquire a sense of peace and that clear state of awareness that went with it, and also the delight of understanding the world from a set of ideas that made it make sense. It is hard to accept that sometimes it doesn't.

Stepping back, what is the aim of the fourth way from the point of view of its basic texts? The most fundamental texts are arguably Ouspensky's *The Psychology of Man's Possible Evolution* and his *In Search of the Miraculous*, also Gurdjieff's *All and Everything*.

Life is only real then, when I am starts with a summary of the intended results of Gurdjieff's *All and Everything*, of which *Life* is the third series. The summary is as follows:

FIRST SERIES: *To destroy, mercilessly, without any compromises whatsoever, in the mentation and feelings of the reader, the beliefs and views, by centuries rooted in him, about everything existing in the world.*

SECOND SERIES: *To acquaint the reader with the material required for a new creation and to prove the soundness and good quality of it.*

THIRD SERIES: *To assist the arising, in the mentation and in the feelings of the reader, of a veritable, nonfantastic representation not of that illusory world which he now perceives, but of the world existing in reality.*[47]

Thus, Gurdjieff is not merely bringing to the West a psychological theory but a full-blown psychological and cosmological revolution. Nevertheless the prologue to *Life is only real then, when I am* begins simply with self-remembering and Gurdjieff's personal difficulty in attaining it at will, at any rate in 1927 by which time he had already been teaching the fourth way system for some time:

---

[47] *Life is only real then, when I am*, p.v

I am...? But what has become of that full-sensing of the whole of myself, formerly always in me in just such cases of self-questioning during the process of self-remembering... . Is it possible that this inner ability was achieved by me thanks to all kinds of self-denial and frequent self-goading only in order that now, when its influence for my Being is more necessary even than air, it should vanish without trace? No! This cannot be! ... Something here is not right![48]

Interestingly that same book is much taken up with the problem that in his absence his teaching had become mis-applied to the point that, "...it seemed clear to me that there stood out on the forehead of now one, now another of you, the inscription 'candidate for the madhouse.'"[49]

The *Psychology* begins with a description of the state of human beings as we find ourselves, that is, without unity, a collection of jostling opinions and feelings each one of which feels entitled to say 'I' at the moment in which it is active. The many 'I's.[50] Most things occur in us mechanically by association, one 'I' to the next. The first lecture contrasts this with the idea of self-remembering, a state in which we can observe these goings on in the mind and also be aware of ourselves and our surroundings. Normally such states are fleeting and infrequent. Ouspensky writes: "The question arises, is it possible to acquire command over these fleeting moments of consciousness, to evoke them more often, and to keep them longer, or even make them permanent? In other words, *is it possible to become conscious?*"[51]

Curiously the rationalist and atheist modern philosopher Daniel Dennett, in his book *Consciousness Explained*, presents a theory which rejects the idea of a central unifying observer and claims that we are a pandemonium (his word) of

---

[48] ibid. p.1

[49] ibid. p.70

[50] Psychology p.15

[51] Psychology pp.21-22, emphasis in the original

different thoughts and tendencies which sort themselves out by some kind of survival of the fittest.[52] In developing this idea he cites Plato's comparison of thoughts to a collection of birds in an aviary.[53] The ancient Greek writer and priest Plutarch also wrote of our multiplicity.[54] So the idea of the many 'I's is not unique to Ouspensky and Gurdjieff. Ouspensky's project, then, is to create observing 'I' as a means towards the unity that both modern psychology and Gurdjieff's system say that we do not have.

While it may be possible and even desirable to achieve greater internal unity, the fourth way goes further. In answer to a question about life after death, Gurdjieff stated that only by certain efforts can a person develop an astral body and that an astral body can survive the death of the physical body, at least for a time. This is connected with the idea of crystallisation, the idea that with sufficient work over time, higher being bodies can become fused, like powder in a retort, and overcome death. In this way self-remembering becomes, not just a method of living more fully here, now, but part of an urgent project of survival. Whether this is plausible or not I shall discuss in what follows.

The development of conscience is also important. Ouspensky wrote, "The aim of this system is to bring man to conscience." He goes on to say, "...what should be understood from the beginning is that a man must have a sense of good and bad. If he has not, nothing can be done for him."

---

[52] Dennett p.222. The word 'pandemonium' combines the Greek words 'pan,' meaning 'all' and 'daimon'—demons or demiurges.

[53] Plato, *Theaetetus* 197-198a

[54] "In fact the Deity is not Many, like each of us who is compounded of hundreds of different factors which arise in the course of our experience, a heterogenous collection combined in a haphazard way. But Being must have Unity, even as Unity must have Being." Plutarch, *The E at Delphi*, in Plutarch *Moralia* 393, Loeb Classical Library volume V, Harvard 1936

Conscience, according to Ouspensky, starts with "ordinary morality" and progresses to realising "the necessity of objective right and wrong"[55] This is achieved through the removal of 'buffers,' that is, what stops us from fully feeling our internal contradictions. In the French language, the word *conscience* refers both to conscience and consciousness.

Perhaps this connects with Socrates's claim that no-one does evil knowingly, that is, if they could see clearly the consequences of what they do, they would do nothing unjust. I emphasise this point, because it means that if your teacher shows evidence of a lack of conscience, then this is an indication that you should look elsewhere.

FOURTH STATE

Fourth state we described in introductory meetings as that state that normally only occurs at times of extreme danger, when time seems to run unusually slowly and there is a calmness and clear-headedness (probably because there is no time to worry or even think). However Ouspensky gives that description for third state.[56]

Whereas third state is sometimes described as the state of being able to be objective about yourself, fourth state is supposedly being objective about the universe.

Ouspensky writes, "In the fourth state of consciousness, that is, in the state of *objective consciousness*, we are supposed to be able to know the full truth *about everything*: we can study 'things in themselves,' 'the world as it is.'"[57]

We used to claim, according to the material in the introductory meetings, that one can, by practicing, be in the third state more and more often, and eventually at will. A person who, by repeated efforts had achieved more-or-less

---

[55] Conscience p.53

[56] Psychology p.21

[57] ibid. p.31, emphasis in the original.

permanent third state might have occasional fourth state experiences.

For me, fourth state is a theory. After twenty-seven years of diligently following the fourth way system I do not know what the fourth state is. If it exists, then I believe it is a defect in the school of which I was a member rather than any lack of effort on my part that I did not experience it. Put it this way: in all that time no-one came up to me and vouchsafed that they could be in fourth state at will or had been in the fourth state, or that the only reason I had not experienced it was that I was doing it all wrong. I only heard of one person, by hearsay, claim to have been in the fourth state. I never heard our teacher refer to it. It may or may not exist.

It is not impossible that you could meet someone from another branch of the fourth way who will claim that they are in and out of fourth state all the time, and will explain to you how to do it. You should at least ask for a time frame on that (see later under 'Time').

Any explorer of higher states of consciousness should bear in mind that all kinds of aberrations and alterations of normal consciousness are possible (like getting drunk) and they are not necessarily 'higher.' My suggestion is that if there exist higher states of consciousness, then one should expect the state to be one of clarity rather than weirdness. Weirdness or anything psychedelic is likely to be an hallucination.

I refer you back to the quotation from Ouspensky: "...in the state of objective consciousness, we are *supposed* to be able to know..." (emphasis mine). He also writes, "As we are not in these [objective] states of consciousness we cannot study these functions or experiment with them, and we learn about them only indirectly from those who have attained or experienced them."[58]

---

[58] *Psychology* p.31

One thing that is clear from this is that Ouspensky was avoiding pretending to knowledge he did not have, at least at the time he produced that material (1937).

It is tempting, when doubting everything, to settle for some certainty in disbelief, to settle for the conclusion that there is no such thing as fourth state or objective consciousness. Ouspensky points out, however, that: "In the religious and philosophical literature of different nations there are many allusions to the higher states of consciousness...."[59] William Blake wrote, "If the doors of perception were cleansed every thing would appear to man as it is, Infinite."[60] Maybe so. At present I have no evidence that the fourth way gets us there, but I like to leave a doubt about doubt. I have not proven that there is no such thing.

It is possible that various states that are sometimes called 'cosmic consciousness' correspond to fourth state. I shall discuss 'cosmic consciousness' and what it might mean later.

MAN NO.S 1, 2, 3

In the fourth way system men and women 1, 2 and 3 are all on the same level. The numbers simply refer to a tendency to operate from one or other of the three 'centres,' moving-instinctive, emotional and intellectual respectively.

It is said to be useful to understand one's 'mechanics,' as these tendencies are referred to, not to judge oneself but quite the reverse, to accept and understand oneself. Do you like parties, prefer to be with friends rather than read a book and you don't enjoy abstract discussions? Fine, you're probably emotionally-centred. You see the world primarily through your emotions. Do you prefer to read a book and you stand awkwardly in the background at dances? You're probably intellectually-centred. And so on. Each of us has situations in which we don't fit in, and feel as though we

---

[59] ibid. p.23

[60] William Blake, The Marriage of Heaven and Hell

should be different from what we are. One of the pieces of advice that was given in the school was not to judge. *Things as they are, myself as I am.* This seems to me to be sound.

Ouspensky advised his students to start with simple self-observation. This is not the same as self-remembering, but is simply observing what one does (what the 'machine' does) without making judgements.

MAN NO.S 4 AND 5

Men and women no. 5 are said to be able to self-remember, that is, to enter into the third state of consciousness at will. It is also said that at any one moment one is either a man or woman 1, 2 or 3 or else a no. 5. One is either 'conscious' (in the sense of third state) or not.

Men and women no. 4 are neither one thing nor the other. They stand at the threshold, or as it were in the doorway, neither in the hallway nor the living room. They are ordinary people who are trying to awaken.

Men and women no. 5 are said to have higher emotional centre working within them. This is said to be a part of us that is dormant unless we awaken. Gurdjieff said that we do not possess a soul, but have to acquire one.

In the Fellowship only two students were alleged to have become men no. 5. One was before my time, and according to reports of others subsequently left the school, and the other was told he was man no. 5 by the teacher during the time when I was a member. When asked about this by another student he simply remarked: 'I record it,' that is, he was trying to make honest observations about what it might mean. Robert Burton asked him, 'Do you feel Influence C pinching you?' to which he replied that he did not. By the Teacher's own account he, the Teacher, was intending to retire at that point and pass on the mantle, however things worked out otherwise and this possible man no. 5 was sidelined in the further history of the school.

Two 'conscious beings' is not a great track record for a school that at its zenith had over two thousand members worldwide, a few of whom have by now been in the school upwards of forty years.

CENTRES OF GRAVITY AND BODY TYPES

You're nothing but a pack of cards!
—Lewis Carroll, *Alice in Wonderland*

I do not recall reading anywhere in Gurdjieff's or Ouspensky's works the idea of body types or centres of gravity. The idea of body types appears to derive from Rodney Collin's *Theory of Celestial Influence* and that of centres of gravity is, as far as I can tell, an innovation by Robert Burton, although I do not know for certain.

In essence both sets of ideas are peripheral to the aim of the fourth way, but they have their uses. Both sets of ideas provide a framework in which one can identify the mechanics of one's 'machine.' This enables one better to understand one's mechanical or automatic reactions to people and situations and thus become more forgiving and accepting of oneself and others.

The idea of centres of gravity appears to be an embellishment on the division of the body into head, heart and guts, or intellectual centre, emotional centre and instinctive-moving centre, which is discussed in *In Search of the Miraculous*. Whereas Ouspensky only talks about these centres in each of us in relation to their basic functions and various speeds, the Fellowship system additionally proposes that each of us operates preferentially from one or more of these centres. In the Fellowship system each of these centres is associated with one of the suits in an ordinary deck of playing cards: clubs for instinctive centre, spades for the moving centre, hearts for the emotional centre and diamonds for the intellectual centre, with each centre further divided into head, heart and guts, or in the Fellowship nomenclature, king, queen and jack.

Thus the moving part of the intellectual centre is the part that free-associates mechanically and stores facts, the emotional part of the intellectual centre is the part that gets excited about new knowledge, and the intellectual part of the intellectual centre can weigh up things intentionally, and can hold an idea without necessarily believing it. The intellectual part of the intellectual centre is called the king of diamonds, the emotional part is the queen and the instinctive-moving part is the jack. Similarly with the other centres, the kings of centres are the parts that can act intentionally, and while these parts do not act consciously as such, they are considered to be the gateway to consciousness and 'higher centres,' symbolised by the jokers.

Each part of each centre is further subdivided into king, queen and jack. Given that each centre is subdivided in this way, each of the four lower centres is divided into a total of nine subdivisions which are designated two to ten.

Specifically the gateway to higher centres is the queen of the king of hearts, that is, the nine of hearts, that is, the emotional part of the intellectual part of the emotional centre. Such is the baroque complexity of Ouspensky's system as embellished through the Fellowship. There is at any rate room for a St Mary figure, if she be the nine of hearts within who gives birth to the conscious being.

So, in terms of the system I am supposed to be intellectually-centred (diamonds), but not the king of diamonds (those rare people who think deeply for what seems ages before answering a question), rather the jack, a collector of random information, a magpie (or perhaps the jack of the queen). You might already have deduced that.

The body type theory derives from Rodney Collin's speculations about the endocrine glands, at least what was known about them in the early 1950s. In *The Theory of Celestial Influence* he lists the endocrine glands that were known at the time (many more hormones have been discovered since) and associates them with the planets. He then places them on

Gurdjieff's enneagram, a nine-pointed diagram arranged around a circle (see next section).

There are of course historical precedents for associating certain character types with the Roman gods and by association with the heavenly bodies, and it is perhaps not an unnatural stretch also to associate character types with endocrine glands. Taking the next step and associating character types with planetary influences is of course highly speculative.

Thus we know what someone means when they talk about a jovial type, someone jocular, good-humoured and tending to the rotund. Jove is another name for Jupiter, father of the Roman gods, and Jupiter is the largest of the planets, with many moons circling it. Thus jovial types attract admirers and hangers-on (although until Galileo no-one knew about Jupiter's moons, and even then Galileo only identified four of them). Examples might include Samuel Johnson who was at the centre of coffee-house intellectual debate in the eighteenth century, or Shakespeare's fictitious character Falstaff. Rodney Collin then associates Jupiter with the anterior pituitary gland, a gland that modulates the activity of a number of other glands, including the thyroid, adrenals, and ovaries.

Similarly we can talk about martial types after Mars, god of war: people of a certain directness and impulsiveness of action. We think of Alexander the Great cutting the Gordian knot with his sword instead of untying it. Collin associates the martial type with the adrenal glands, source of the 'fight or flight' hormone adrenaline. Similarly Rodney Collin manages to associate other types, lunar, mercurial, venusian and so on with various of the endocrine glands, some more plausibly than others.

Advisers in psychology and business sometimes use other classifications of type, such as other variations on Gurdjieff's enneagram, or the entirely different Myers-Briggs classification. However such classifications are based on observation of manifestations only and so are bound to be somewhat arbitrary and circular. Lunar types tend to be solitary and introverted. Because I tend to be solitary and introverted I am a lunar type. There is nothing underpinning this, unless the link with the endocrine glands is correct, for which I know of no evidence whatever (the lunar type is supposed to be associated with the pancreas—I'm not sure why—insulin puts sugar back in the cells as lunars go back in their shells?). There is even less reason to suppose that the endocrine glands are under the influence of the planets. But as a way of helping us accept ourselves and others as we are, it has its uses.

From childhood I was shy and under-confident and even as a much more confident adult I do not mix easily with others. I find small-talk difficult and it is a skill I have had to acquire through effort and practice. Thus to understand that this is simply my 'type' was something of a relief. My type is neither good nor bad, just one of many. As the song says, 'I am who I'm meant to be, this is me.'

As with the 'centres of gravity,' such classifications can be helpful but in my view not essential, curiosities perhaps useful at times. No type is said to be superior to any other in terms of spiritual understanding, but it may determine what we love and what we seem naturally good at.

Up to a point there is some truth in the idea of centres of gravity and perhaps body types, but I do not think that should pre-determine one's fate. That I am not instinctively centred may account for why I am not a chef, but that does not stop me from learning to cook meals that are accounted tasty by my family. I have seen a class of children learning to dance and it is obvious by the age of four or five which ones already seem to have dancing in them and which are a little awkward. Even so I saw one who at age ten seemed lacking in grace, two years on perform a solo with considerable beauty. Sufficient love of something and sufficient effort can produce surprising results.

THE ENNEAGRAM

The *enneagram*, Gurdjieff's diagram of nine points, has been subsequently adopted by all kinds of people to classify supposed relationships between things, not always with any obvious connection with the diagram as originally set out.

I am principally familiar with it as a diagram of the relationships between the various body types, and as a way of understanding our different essences it is as good as any. Classifying ourselves and each other in this way can help in understanding our 'mechanics,' why we do things in particular characteristic ways, that we are not unique, and that our differences from other types need not result in self-deprecation or negative judgements of others. We are what we are.

Rodney Collin claimed that there is a circulation within the enneagram, such that each body type tends towards the next one in the flow of the diagram. Thus a lunar type, during the course of spiritual evolution, will tend to become more venusian, venusians will become more mercurial, and so on. This is another of those ideas that seem to lack evidence.

A curiosity is that the flow inside the enneagram is the same as the decimal expansion of one seventh, that is, 0.142857 recurring: all the digits except 3, 6 and 9.

THE FOOD DIAGRAM

To awaken, the fourth way system of Gurdjieff and Ouspensky says we need to accumulate *higher hydrogens*.

Here in a few words is the scheme:

By repeated efforts over a long period of time it is possible to wake up fully, to become conscious in the terms of the System;

Through self-remembering one accumulates *higher hydrogens*—finer substances which crystallise in one—in this process consciousness can be made permanent;

Beyond a certain level of attainment, what has been gained cannot be lost, and that person becomes effectively immortal.

To accumulate higher hydrogens the various foods are transformed by the mechanism of the body, seen as a factory. There are three food types: ordinary food, air and impressions. Ordinary food is transformed into finer substances by air (corresponding to the various chemical processes of digestion and assimilation), and finer substances still are formed from the two *conscious shocks, self-remembering* and *voluntary suffering*. Every day the organism is given or generates enough energy to accumulate finer substances, eventually to build a soul, but ordinarily this energy is wasted in unnecessary talk and the expression of negative emotions.

All this relates to the *food diagram*, which is explained in detail in *In Search of the Miraculous*. Further elaboration is to be found in Beckwith's *Ouspensky's Fourth Way*.[61]

What can we make of these finer substances? And what are we to make of the claim that acquiring a soul will make us immortal?

HIGHER HYDROGENS

In *In Search of the Miraculous* Ouspensky discusses Gurdjieff's concept of 'hydrogens,' the idea that the universe is composed of different orders of substance, the finer interpenetrating the coarser. According to Gurdjieff, everything, even the Absolute is material, but a very fine type of material. These finer types of substance, or *higher hydrogens*, are unknown to modern science.[62]

A friend once light-heartedly asked whether in California it was possible to buy higher hydrogens in a jar. I suppose if there were anywhere on the planet where you could buy

---

[61] *In Search of the Miraculous* pp.182-192; Beckwith pp. 222-232

[62] *In Search of the Miraculous* pp.86-90

higher hydrogens in a jar it would be California. Of course if we adopt a materialist world view then we feel as though higher hydrogens ought to be something we could somehow see or feel or otherwise demonstrate the existence of in some physical way.[63]

However I have another take on this.

We experience many real things that do not have a recognised chemical structure, like the emotions of aesthetic experience or sexual attraction, for example. We can be in low moods or light states, and sometimes our states of mind can be changed by places, like a fine garden or the sea. Sometimes, when in the kind of love that invades us, usually but not always in youth, the whole world is transformed into a place infused with painful wonder.[64] We might I suppose try, as some have, to link various emotional states with various brain neurotransmitters. But it is more natural to think of the whole experience of the garden and our state of mind as one thing, as though somehow the feeling of the garden and the feeling evoked by it shared the same substance. We even say, metaphorically, 'there must be something in the air.' Somehow the explanation that it is just an increase of serotonin, endorphins or whatever in the brain doesn't really feel as though it explains anything. (In any event, I don't think neuroscientists would seriously claim that it's that simple.)

Considering that Gurdjieff's system supposedly came from Central Asia in the 19th century, and may possibly derive from a Sufi tradition a few hundred years old, that is, long before the chemists of the eighteenth century, then it would

---

[63] Most of the matter in the universe is so-called 'dark matter' which we also cannot buy in a jar in California or anywhere else, but there is no reason to think either that it is a higher hydrogen or that it doesn't exist, although we don't know what it is.

[64] 'Pains of love be sweeter far than all other pleasures are.' Dryden (1631-1700), Ah, how sweet it is to love!

not be unnatural for the thinkers of those earlier times to attribute the states evoked by people and places to finer or coarser substances.

We have already considered that the kinds of concept that we use to describe biological phenomena are quite different from the concepts that physicists use in describing the atomic and subatomic worlds. We are usually content to use yet other types of language to discuss painting or music. So there is no reason in principle why quite other concepts than those of ordinary chemistry should not be useful in describing (for example) states of being evoked by landscapes, people, food, works of art, buildings or books.

It seems to me that there is some sense in classifying things according to their 'hydrogen' or the 'world' they belong to (see next section), although Gurdjieff never explained to Ouspensky why he used the term hydrogen. Nevertheless Ouspensky is clear that Gurdjieff's view is that the whole universe is material, and that there are different degrees of matter, some finer than others, which are not recognised by modern science. While we may recognise the states, it is difficult to know how one would verify that these states are related to actual substances, as opposed to the more conventional view that these states represent different relationships between things and our perceptions of them.

One implication of the theory that these states are underpinned by actual subtle substances is that it opens up the possibility of life after the death of the physical body. That is, when the body composed of hydrogen 48 drops away, a body within it composed of hydrogen 24 might somehow persist. However for this we are offered no evidence.

HIGHER WORLDS

The idea of hydrogens is related to the idea of worlds. The worlds are designated by numbers, which relate to the idea that each world or level of existence is under a certain number of laws. The finer worlds are said to be under fewer laws.

Nowhere in the literature have I come across any explanation of what these laws are, and the questions of new students about that were usually brushed off with some vague waffle which I don't remember. Even so there is some intuitive sense to the idea. When we are awake we are able to accomplish a lot more than when dreaming, and when cured of some neurotic compulsion or fear we are freer than before. We are under fewer laws, so to speak (for example, the law that you must cower behind the furniture until a spider is removed from the room).

World 48 is characterised as a normal, ordinary state, neither high nor low, like a blank piece of paper. World 96 is the world of coarse impressions. World 24 is the state of essence, the child-like, guileless state of simplicity and wonder. World 12 is essence together with awakened consciousness. World 12 impressions are said to be rare. One student had the opinion that Andrei Rublev's ikon of the three angels who visited Abraham is a World 12 impression.

FOOD FOR THE MOON

Everything eats and is eaten, Gurdjieff tells us. After death our energy goes to the Moon, which belongs to world 96.

According to Gurdjieff there are two streams: a descending stream in which energy flows from the Absolute outwards into creation, and a much smaller ascending stream which flows upwards, back towards the origin. The stream is called the *ray of creation*. It is the job of those who choose to be in the Work to join the smaller, upward-flowing stream.

The moon is supposedly at the end of the ray of creation. It will gradually evolve to become more like the earth, and the earth in turn will gradually evolve towards becoming a sun. The moon is supposedly fed by the souls of those who swim in the downward, outward stream.[65]

---

[65] In *Search of the Miraculous* pp.83,85

There is nothing in modern physics to suggest that a body like the earth could ever be massive enough to become a star. The sun has about a million times more mass than the earth and its heat and light are powered by fusion reactions involving hydrogen (the kind of hydrogen that conventional physics knows about). The earth has relatively little hydrogen in elemental form and is too small ever to be a sun. The moon is too small to retain much of an atmosphere and there is no known mechanism by which it could somehow grow, short of accumulating an enormous number of impacts with asteroids. In defence of Ouspensky, the idea that the sun might be powered by nuclear fusion was first suggested in 1920 by Sir Arthur Eddington, and that the most abundant element in the sun was hydrogen was not discovered until 1925 by Cecilia Payne and was ignored, partly, one suspects, because Payne was a woman.[66] Gurdjieff's cosmology fitted, almost, if you didn't think about it too hard, into a gap in contemporary understanding, although it should still have strained the credulity of an educated person at the time.

How did I come to believe it? I didn't. I accepted without challenge that descending souls would end up in the moon and thought no more about it. It was never central to why I was there and I gave it very little thought. I never thought seriously about the idea that the earth might become a sun, and I never for a moment accepted Ouspensky's belief that humans are not descended from apes.[67] My focus was very much on awakening.

If the cosmology of the fourth way is to make any sense at all, it has to be taken as some kind of allegory, because taken at face value it is fantastical.

---

[66] Lucie Green, 15 Million Degrees, Viking Penguin 2016 p.47

[67] Psychology p.10

FEMININE DOMINANCE

This is not a name I have found in the fourth way literature, and I think it is an innovation by Robert Burton. *Feminine dominance* is the force that keeps us doing what we are doing, in other words, that keeps us mechanical. I think somewhere Gurdjieff refers to a similar idea as the *general law*. I don't know why Robert Burton called it *feminine dominance*.

On a cosmic level it is 'what keeps the planets in their orbits' (what ordinary folk call the laws of physics). On a personal level it is doing what is expected of us, whether or not such behaviour is in our interest or in the interest of others.

Once I was on holiday with my family in Cornwall and we met a couple who had recently moved there (not, as far as I was aware, belonging to any kind of esoteric school). The husband explained that he had once been on a course and part of the learning experience was to increase personal freedom by acting against what people expect and trying not to be affected by it. The exercise involved pulling a banana on a string through the street. Apparently he had accomplished this. Anyway, our two families decided to attend a meeting in the town which was advertised as a brief presentation by the bank followed by cheese and wine. Free cheese and wine, we thought, so we went. The presentation was so unutterably boring and so protracted that after a while I realised that we were all sitting there because of this 'general law,' since frankly the cheese and wine would not compensate for it. I reminded our new friend about the banana and finally we all left.

On the one hand it is good to be able to do what is right irrespective of what other people think. On the other hand some seem to interpret it as giving *carte blanche* to all kinds of barely legal behaviour. 'Going against feminine dominance' can lead to a feeling that illegal activity is acceptable. Once a student was in danger of losing his driver's licence because of a repeat speeding offence. He asked students in the 'good householder' part of a meeting whether anyone would say that they had been driving his car on the day in question, thus acquiring the extra points but not being banned. I had to point out to him that this was fraud and not something that anyone with any sense would indulge in. I also came across a number of marriages which looked as though they might have to do with immigration to the United States. Also, many of the developments at the headquarters of the Fellowship were allegedly done without proper planning permission, and covered up from aerial view by the positioning of prodigious numbers of palm trees.

It can be ethically correct to break the law for the sake of a compelling moral imperative, usually only in extreme circumstances. If breaking the law results in one's own advantage one should question one's motivation.

THE LAW OF SEVEN

The law of seven tells us that all events proceed in steps corresponding to the notes in the musical octave. Ouspensky explains that each octave has two intervals, corresponding to the semitones between mi and fa and between si and do. At the intervals extra energy is required to bridge the interval, otherwise the octave takes a new direction. Ouspensky says that unless this intentional energy is put in at the intervals, an octave is likely to deviate, and if this pattern is repeated one can end up doing almost the opposite of what one first intended. "This law shows why straight lines never occur in our activities, why, having begun to do one thing, we in fact constantly do something entirely different, often the opposite of the first, although we do not notice this and continue to think that we are doing the same thing that we began to do."[68]

We can all think of activities that begin with enthusiasm, like starting to learn a new language, and then hit an

---

[68] In *Search of the Miraculous* pp.128-9

inevitable interval where difficulty dominates and progress seems almost to stop. We despair of ever achieving anything close to fluency. Only dogged determination, or the encouragement of a friend or a good teacher can take us beyond the interval into further progress. That is, there needs to be what Ouspensky called a 'parallel octave' or an external shock to help the first octave bridge its interval.

On a political level there have been events like the Russian revolution, the effects of which Ouspensky was all too familiar with, taking its justification from relieving the oppression of the proletariat and resulting in one of the most murderous oppressions in history. This is an example of setting out to do one thing and ending up doing the opposite. An example of a parallel octave might be a country with an independent judiciary. The existence of an independent judiciary can, with good will and vigilance, keep a government on the straight and narrow path when it might otherwise degenerate into a tyranny. The one octave proceeding normally can sustain the other past the interval.

Critics of the Fellowship might see the same law at work, with the interval not being bridged. I would go further and say that from my perspective it felt like a *descending octave*.

Although the idea of intervals fits everyday events very well, I have not met anyone who could explain the significance of the other notes in the octave, what it might mean to be at *sol* or *la* in an activity.

THE LAW OF THREE

According to the law of three, nothing can take place without a third force. For every event there is first force which initiates the activity, second or denying force which opposes it, and third force which allows it to happen.

In the morning when the alarm radio comes on, I remember I must get up for work. I still feel tired because I am not a morning person, so I stay in bed a few more minutes. Finally something changes and I find my body moving out of bed almost without my willing it. Is it that the first thing I am going to do is make coffee, and the coffee happens to be very good? I'm not actually sure what the third force is, but something has broken the impasse.

Rodney Collin and Francis Roles developed the idea of three forces into the six processes, in which the three forces interact in different ways.[69]

I cannot in honesty say that this idea has been particularly practical in my life. I suppose, though, if something isn't working it is reasonable to ask what third force could be brought to bear on it to allow things to progress in the desired direction. It might be something as simple as a phone call or a smile.

INTENTIONAL INSINCERITY

Intentional insincerity is a term used in the Fellowship meaning 'the practice, in order to further one's aim, of saying something which is not strictly true in circumstances where it will not cause real harm to anyone.'[70]

It is an idea I have never had any time for, even in the depths of belief. I have known students to use it for some lower aim as though to deceive 'life' people is perfectly legitimate. It isn't. It is a tool used to further the aims of what the School calls 'the lower self.'

At most, I would avoid mentioning the School and my involvement in it, but this was not difficult because almost nobody was interested in any case.

I have always seen dishonesty as a way unnecessarily to complicate life and to put one's relation to reality at one remove. It is to be avoided by anyone who does not wish to have to waste energy on fabrications. A direct and open relation to the truth is necessary for inner tranquility.

---

[69] The Theory of Celestial Influence, pp.172-203
[70] Girard Haven, Creating a soul, p. 596

THE ARK

Here as always I must, for the sake of avoiding self-deception, record my own gullibility. In my early days in the School it was suggested that one could regard oneself as if one were an interesting stranger. With a little effort I can perhaps succeed in this, recording my weaknesses without either indulging in guilt or making myself look better than I am.

Early on in the School I was aware of Robert's prediction that sooner or later nuclear armageddon would occur. This came as no surprise to me, since before meeting the School (or even realising that I wanted to find one) I had been active in the peace movement. The Cuban missile crisis (1962) was in the news when I was a child old enough to understand. In the eighties and nineties an escalating arms race made nuclear war frighteningly likely, with the already dangerous doctrine of Mutually Assured Destruction (MAD—as satirised in Kubrik's film Dr Strangelove) being made obsolete by more accurate weapons and by President Ronald Reagan's Star Wars programme, which could potentially make a first strike look like a viable option for a paranoid government.

In 1990 I had travelled with IPPNW (International Physicians for the Prevention of Nuclear War) and a small delegation from the Western Shoshone Nation to Moscow and Kazakhstan, in order to protest at nuclear weapons testing and to push for a global nuclear test ban treaty. I suspect that we were being played, both by Eduard Shevardnadze (then Soviet Foreign Minister) and by local Kazakh politicians, while at the same time we were ignored in the West (apart from a letter I wrote which was published in the European). I came away disillusioned with the peace movement: not that it was not well-intentioned, but that it was ineffective. I felt that real change had to begin at the human rather than the political level. I had heard the six-handshakes theory, which holds that every human being is no more than six handshakes from any other. Real change must start with work on oneself. It was in the following year that I joined the School.

Early on a student told me in hushed tones Robert's prediction about nuclear war. The idea was that in exchange for esoteric knowledge, Influence C requires a payment, and that payment is the creation of an Ark so that civilisation can survive a nuclear war. While the idea of an Ark in relation to a global catastrophe was not something I had known about before, it did not surprise me. If anything I was more surprised by the way other students 'buffered' the topic— people do not like to think about what the real consequences of nuclear war would be—a topic I had read about in some detail. The student, a kindly elderly lady, added that the birthmark on Gorbachev's forehead indicated, according to Robert, that Russia would suffer 'a direct hit.'

When I later visited Apollo (then Renaissance) it did occur to me that it was totally unprepared. The School did not measure up as a survivalist organisation at all, and my rationalisation for this was that, after all, the main purpose of a school of awakening is awakening, not the strengthening of the instinctive part. It seemed to me that Robert's various predictions were aimed at reminding us of our mortality and of the impermanence of the things we become attached to, the better to bring us to appreciation of the present moment, the only thing we have for certain.

I think it was probably in 2006 that I was in Apollo (then named Isis for the Egyptian goddess and before the terrorist organisation of that name was heard of). This was the year that Robert first predicted the fall of California (he did again later). I was sitting next but one to him at one of the dinners held in the formal garden at the back of the Galleria (now the Academy). I remember Robert saying, 'I am so excited!' He was actually looking forward to the event, when he assumed that Apollo would be spared and would become a coastal city. It did cross my mind at the time that such a catastrophe would involve millions of drowned and that to be looking forward to it was an inappropriate emotion. But I did not question Robert as a teacher. At a similar dinner not long afterwards, when California had failed to fall into the sea, Robert referred to an item of news that there had been a large earthquake in Iran. He said that Iran was on the opposite side of the world to California and took this as a sign from Influence C that the prediction was partly right. Both California and Iran are north of the equator, San Francisco at 37.8N and Iran (Luristan) at 33.4N. For there to be any correspondence the longitudes would have to be separated by 180 degrees. California (San Francisco) is 122.4W and Iran (Luristan) is 48.4E, making a separation of 170.8 degrees. I did look at a map but I didn't do the sums, and I accepted it, wide-eyed, in the way Robert intended.

It is hard to believe any more in the idea of Apollo or the School being an Ark given that the School population is ageing and the world-wide membership is diminishing.

The preparedness of Apollo for nuclear war was always close to non-existent. Beale Air Force Base is a United States Air Force base located approximately 12 miles south of Apollo, and would be an obvious target for incoming nuclear missiles in the event of an all-out nuclear conflict. An airburst would probably be sufficient to ground any planes that are dependent on modern electronic equipment (presumably all of them) because of EMP (electromagnetic pulse) effects alone, and this would not cause radiation fallout. However a ground-burst could not be ruled out. Either way, electricity would be knocked out in Apollo and it is likely that motor vehicles would also be affected as well as any other equipment dependent on microchips. A car with an old-fashioned carburettor and choke might still work as long as there was petrol, however the delivery of petrol would no doubt cease and the pumps would not work if the electricity was cut off.

Most water at Apollo is pumped up from wells tens of feet underground. In the event that the electricity grid went down, getting water would become an immediate problem. Pumps would have to run on fuels other than electricity unless the electricity were generated locally. There are a number of small lakes on the property at Apollo, but no natural irrigation.

Wildfires would be likely, depending on the time of year. Even without a war, wildfires have been devastating. The town of Paradise some 56km (35 miles) north-west of Apollo was completely destroyed by such a fire in November 2018.

In the event of a ground-burst there would be considerable radiation and the level at Apollo would depend on the wind direction. I heard that there was the thought of using the winery as a fallout shelter. There is some plausibility to that, given that it is a large concrete structure, but survivors would have to remain indoors for at least two weeks to avoid significant radiation exposure. There would have been plenty of wine in 2006, although now the wine is being sold off. There are now a number of animals including turkeys and camels, so there might be sufficient meat for a while.

In an all-out nuclear war, a nuclear winter would probably follow, similar to or worse than the volcanic winter following the eruption of Mount Tambora in 1815, which was followed by 'the year without a summer' and global food shortages. Obtaining food would become a problem, and all food would have to be sourced locally.

All of this was apparent to me even during the time of my committed membership, however I rationalised it. First, it was explicit that the Fellowship was not a survivalist organisation, and that its prime purpose was the awakening of its students. Too much attention to the details of physical survival too soon would encourage identification with the instinctive centre. There was no stockpiling of food and there were no caches of armaments or any reference to training in firearms (the owning of firearms was banned in the Fellowship in 1980). Second, I assumed that should there be a disaster (and I made no efforts to move to Apollo in anticipation of it) that Influence C would somehow take care of it. Third, I assumed that Robert made these predictions in order to remind students not to identify too much with present material gains, since in the end all is wiped away. In sum, for my own part I did not analyse too closely the contradictions implicit in the predictions. Robert has said that Schools do not make sense, a point underlined by the later arrival of the camels to Apollo. The predictions certainly did not make sense.

As regards the anticipated fall of California in 2018, one student posted a warning notice in the post office nearest the Fellowship's headquarters in California, but Robert Burton was reportedly not happy about it. There is a kind of callous madness that results from the System, at least as it was understood in the Fellowship.

REASON

In returning to Ouspensky's writings it becomes clear to me how much of the absurdity that crept into my beliefs does not belong to Ouspensky. It is as though a plain earthenware jar had dropped into the sea and become so encrusted in barnacles and calcified worm casts as to be transformed into something not merely rich and strange, but barely recognisable.

Some of the fourth way writings, particularly of Ouspensky, contain perceptive observations about our human psychology, the ways in which it goes wrong, and what can be done about it. Some of these insights are quite different from those of conventional psychology, whether from Freud, Jung, modern behaviourism or even humanistic psychotherapy. Also, some of the things said by Gurdjieff about the chaotic state of the world as run by 'sleeping beings' (living as he did through the Armenian genocide, the Russian revolution and World War 1) are as relevant today as when he said them. Clever yet morally idiotic dictators are common, as are their lackeys. Other ideas, particularly some of those taken as truths in the organisation of which I was a part, are in hindsight so obviously groundless that I wonder how I came to accept them, ideas whose credibility dispersed like smoke in a breeze within days of leaving.

In *The Psychology of Man's Possible Evolution* there are turns of phrase that show when Ouspensky is talking about things that are for him only theories. He writes for example about what the fourth state of consciousness is *supposed* to be, yet he does not use that kind of phrase when discussing self-remembering. He is careful, in other words, not to lie. Lying in relation to psychology, he explains, "*means speaking about* things one does not know, and even cannot know, as though one knows and can know."[71]

It is all the more curious, then, that Ouspensky is so taken with what he has heard from Gurdjieff that he repeats much that he did not claim to have verified, and even what Ouspensky says we cannot verify. His honesty prevents him claiming these as things he knows, and yet he passes them on as part of a system to be followed. It is clear in the *Psychology* that he is in the process of setting up school work based on Gurdjieff's teaching, perhaps with the justification that if what he *does* understand works, what he doesn't understand will presumably turn out to be true as well. If the apples you buy in the market are good, will you not return to the same stall next time and even buy their oranges as well? (That was also my excuse.)

I invite the reader to consider that nothing that he or she has not verified for him or herself is to be considered true, at any rate when it comes to spiritual and psychological teachings. Yet I myself entered 'the Work' with just that caveat and I still ended up, like Ouspensky, believing what I had no way of knowing.

In our introductory meetings it was a standard part of the script to say, 'do not believe or disbelieve anything you hear tonight.' The point is that allowing the critical mind to start taking ideas apart before they've even been heard properly can prevent one from hearing anything genuinely new. It is a point made by Ouspensky himself: "...when we hear new things, we take them for the old, or think they can be explained and interpreted by the old."[72]

That does not mean that once one has made a sincere effort to understand and apply new ideas, critical thought should be abandoned. It remains an essential tool in its right use.

---

[71] *Psychology* p.41, emphasis in the original.

[72] *Psychology* p.6

REASON CAN TAKE YOU TO THE DOOR

It is said that reason can take you to the door, but it cannot take you through.

Parmenides (5th-6th century BC), according to his own account, arrived at the door and was guided through by a goddess. When he had understood that all is One he called this understanding the Way of Truth, and the ordinary sciences he called the Way of Opinion. Nevertheless he wrote a whole book about the Way of Opinion (that is to say, what we normally think of as knowledge), which is now lost.

The fourth way puts the intellectual centre in the lower centres. The instinctive-moving, emotional and intellectual centres are all described as part of the 'machine.' Consciousness itself belongs to higher emotional and intellectual centres according to the System. From this can arise the downplaying of the value of reason, albeit reason intentionally applied is said to belong to the highest part of the intellectual centre.

It is I believe correct that the analytic mind cannot of itself enter into the present moment. The intellect is an organ of thought rather than of experience. I concede of course that everything that happens, necessarily happens in the present moment, including analytic thought. But all words and symbols are substitutes for reality. They are counters that enable us to calculate and maps that show us the way, but are not the destination.

To live in the moment is to take in the impressions of things around one. It is likely that those impressions are instantly interpreted and conditioned by thought, but thought and awareness are two different things, as Ouspensky pointed out.[73] Consciousness is one thing, functions are another. While it may well be impossible to receive any impression without interpreting it at some level, it is possible to train oneself to see and hear more clearly

---

[73] *Psychology* p.17

what is there rather than what one thinks is there. This is what you have to do if you want to learn to draw realistic pictures, for example, or to really hear birdsong while letting the thought, 'that's the song of a blackbird' drop into the background. We can learn not to have our waking moments 'sicklied o'er with the pale cast of thought.'[74] The experience of awe, for example silently watching the mist rise from a lake at dawn, can be had without words.

THE SLEEP OF REASON

There was a definite tendency in the Fellowship, encouraged by Burton, to abandon reason altogether and simply plunge into the present moment. At least that is what I infer from the abandonment of student *angles*—contributions from our own experience—in the big teaching events, and the absence also of questions in those events. Only new students in the peripheral centres seemed to have questions, although when I first joined it was said that if you didn't have questions, you weren't working. It was also a key part of my early acceptance of working in the Fellowship that I didn't have to believe anything, and that the Work was empirical and practical: you tried the exercises to see what would happen, to verify what had been taught. This is also stated by Gurdjieff: "No 'faith' is required on the fourth way; on the contrary faith of any kind is opposed to the fourth way."[75] Emptying the mind should not be a recipe for then filling it with all kinds of nonsense.

In a pure scientific experiment one should not aim to verify anything. Rather, a good experiment should be set up in order to attempt, as far as possible, to disprove a theory, especially if it's a theory you rather like. The tougher the test, the more confidence we can have in a theory that survives it. Another way of doing good science is to set up an investigation so that the outcome is going to be interesting

---

[74] Shakespeare, *Hamlet* Act 3 scene 1
[75] In *Search of the Miraculous* p. 49

either way. However, in the area of personal psychology or spirituality, whatever you want to call it, one does have a definite aim, one is not neutral in relation to the outcome. It is an applied science, not a pure one. The fourth way arguably is more like an applied science or art, in which one is using methods already established for a particular purpose. However, since there are many methods, ways, gurus and so on, many of which are doubtful or even harmful, one cannot place one's trust in any of them wholeheartedly, but ought to retain a certain healthy skepticism, even while diligently applying the methods.

A better comparison therefore would be if you wanted to learn to play the violin. You would do the scales and bow exercises with the aim of being able to play, and you would practice a great deal. That doesn't mean that you would abandon critical thought and place your entire unreserved trust in your teacher. You would still appraise your progress both with regard to your own efforts and with regard to the ability of your teacher to teach you. It may be that your teacher would never let you down. But there is a necessary balance.

My experience of being in the Fellowship was that independent thought was not encouraged. It was not that thinking was forbidden, rather that one simply tended to confine both one's exploratory and critical thinking to areas that did not challenge the teaching, and to investigations that enhanced and bolstered the existing orthodoxy. There was a strong element of 'Robert said,' the fallacy of believing un-evidenced statements because the Teacher says so.

In the Fellowship, knowledge was increasingly derived from signs and portents in the art of the past and in mundane events. But knowledge is not the right word. What was found in the art and writings of the past and in portents was simply the same message presented in different ways, and that message was the Sequence, a mantra composed of six single-syllable Work 'I's invented by the teacher. At this point, in my view, the teaching as presented had all but died and the school was continuing simply under its own momentum, as a train might that had run out of steam but not applied the brakes. Even so, for some years I continued as a regularly participating member. Once or twice I subscribed to the transcripts of the teacher's meetings but on each occasion did not renew, and read very little of them. All the interesting ideas had gone out of them. I told myself that the Work was not intended to appeal to my intellect. But the truth was that what the Teacher had to say at that time was no longer 'emotional' either. It seemed that he had run out of things to say.

At some point in 2019, after I had left, an edict went out from the Teacher to dispose of all fourth way books and writings made prior to that time (an edict rapidly withdrawn), as though members were all so far advanced that they no longer needed the System but only the word of the Teacher. Certainly the art of dispassionate reason had been lost.

The function of the intellect is to gather evidence and also act like a surgeon's knife, removing what is wrong. Reason can tell a valid argument from a false one, including distinguishing claims that are evidenced from claims that are mere unsupported pronouncements. It is true that reason cannot create anything genuinely new, any more than you can have a logical argument without premises. But removing the unnecessary is as vital as having the rubbish taken away. It massively enhances the value of what is left.

THE PROBLEM OF RECEIVED KNOWLEDGE

Robert Burton claimed that in the sequence of the nine lives of an ascending soul one would only once be born a woman. Meher Baba said that alternate lives are male and female.[76] Clearly both cannot be true, unless Meher Baba was only

---

[76] Meher Baba, *God to man and man to God*, Sheriar Press 1975, p.190

referring to reincarnation in general but not to the last nine lives, which for some reason he doesn't mention. In general it is possible to find differences of opinion regarding such arcane matters between different sources, even when, as in the case of the Fellowship, all of the sources are said to be awakened.

I read in the Sushruta Samhita, an ancient Indian medical treatise, a list of the sources of knowledge. From memory these included direct observation, learning from a teacher, divine inspiration and learning from authority. For practical purposes one has no choice for the most part in trusting authoritative sources and teachers. In reading this essay you presumably place some (I hope guarded) faith in what I write even though you have not experienced all of it yourself. But since authorities and teachers can contradict one another, in the end deciding between conflicting claims depends on personal verification, or at least the balance of probability when judged from other reliable sources.

An additional problem presents itself when the subject matter has no obvious means of verification. What conceivable investigation could one do to discover whether alternate lives of an ascending soul were male and female? It may be that Meher Baba was speaking from his knowledge of some ancient tradition, or perhaps from a memory of his own past lives. But what credence can we put on that, if other traditions (say, the Bible or the Koran) make no mention of it?

If we were to assume that Meher Baba was right, given that he is one of the forty-four conscious beings listed by Robert Burton and so has as much right to authoritative statements as any other, what mental process would lead Burton to express a different view? My best guess is that he made a back-of-the-envelope probability calculation based on his belief that only one of the forty-four was a woman (Queen Elizabeth I).

In general claims about things that are impossible to verify even in principle ought to be treated as without meaningful content. There is nothing you can usefully do with such claims.

A NEW MUDDLE OF THE UNIVERSE

In all this reassessment of my beliefs, my model of the universe has been radically altered, yet in some sense remains the same.

While in the School I held two different views of the nature of the world, one 'spiritual' and the other materialistic. It was not that these views were in sealed separate compartments, but that I was always looking for the place where they joined. Emotionally I still am.

On the one hand there was the model that had been inculcated into me through a very thorough conventional education. On the other was a feeling that the essence of the universe was consciousness itself, or God, or The Absolute. I was between Democritus and Parmenides, atomism and pantheism. I read Ibn 'Arabi's *Whoso knoweth himself knoweth his Lord* just before I joined the Fellowship. For Ibn 'Arabi there is nothing that is not God.

Followers of Gurdjieff and Ouspensky might point out that Gurdjieff stated that everything is material, even God, but the materiality of God is of a different order than that of ordinary matter.[77] But as discussed in the section on higher hydrogens, there is no obvious way of demonstrating these finer substances, and if they are taken as metaphors then unfortunately we are left with God as a metaphor, which is unsatisfactory.

My education included the standard understanding of physics and chemistry up to pre-university level, and how the constituents of matter and their properties were discovered by experiment.

---

[77] In Search of the Miraculous p.86

I had also read an account of how Galileo showed that a one pound and a ten pound weight both fall at the same rate, that there were irregularities on the surface of the moon, that there are other moons circling other planets, and that the accepted belief at the time that blood gets from one side to the other side of the heart through minute holes in the septum between the ventricles was simply wrong. All of these conclusions were got from observation. Weights can be dropped from the leaning tower of Pisa and timed. The face of the moon can be seen through a telescope (invented in the Netherlands by Hans Lippershey in 1608). There are no holes in the septum of the heart in healthy people. The novelised account that I read had Galileo confronting an anatomist who failed to demonstrate the holes while still believing in them.[78]

During my education I was taught about how incautious interpretation of facts can deceive. That A happens with B

---

[78] An up-to-date example: a 2018 article in the on-line medical publication Medscape describes a debate in front of an audience of cardiologists about whether putting stents in partially-blocked coronary arteries is a useful procedure. One doctor presented the evidence from a large well-conducted trial that stents do not improve symptoms of angina except by a placebo effect, do not reduce the likelihood of a further heart attack, and do not reduce mortality. The doctor speaking for stents, instead of criticising the study or producing other evidence, showed slides of partially-blocked arteries and appealed to emotions—"What if this were your coronary artery?" A show of hands at the end of the debate showed that the majority were still convinced that stents are a useful modality of treatment of coronary artery disease. So even highly-trained minds can be deceived if their emotions over-ride their reason.
(https://www.medscape.com/viewarticle/895945? nlid=122102_4663&src=WNL_mdplsnews_180504_mscpedit_fmed& uac=264161MJ&spon=34&impID=1624424&faf=1#vp_2)

does not prove that A causes B, because both could be caused by something else.

As Galileo experienced to his cost, upsetting the powers of that time, and as we observed with the emerging evidence in the 20th century that smoking causes lung cancer, upsetting the tobacco industry, there is strong resistance to the facts in anyone with a vested interest in believing otherwise: in the 17th century it was the Church, and in the 20th the tobacco companies and the doctors in their pay. You do not have to be in a cult to believe things that are unreasonable or highly implausible.

Nevertheless the idea of a magical universe has also always appealed to me. I remember trying to explain to a student who was on the point of leaving and could no longer relate to Robert's interpretation of signs, that Robert was trying to teach us a new way of experiencing the world, of being able to understand its language. I felt that indeed there were 'tongues in trees, books in the running brooks, sermons in stones, and good in every thing' as Shakespeare has it.[79] Being present can lead to a peaceful state of mind in which everything does seem illuminated and wonderful, and one's own existence in it strange. But probably the student found Robert's interpretations of number plates and signs improbable, strained and banal. I would now agree.

But there is magic in presence.

I tried, intellectually, to square the circle between the material and the magical. Physics, I realised, has no definition of 'now.' Physics deals with time, space, mass, energy, fields and so on, and of course it is possible to specify specific places and times in relation to others, but nothing in physics privileges one place or moment over another. Yet for each living being 'now' is unique—as well as constantly changing.

---

[79] As You Like It, Act II, scene i, lines 1–17

This observation, intriguing as it appears, has not led me to any startling breakthroughs. Some would argue that everything is consciousness and our separateness in the material world an illusion, however I find my separateness, if it is an illusion, remarkably convincing. That theory lacks content in the sense of failing to supply any testable predictions.

Equally I do not find the idea that one day there will be a materialistic explanation of consciousness convincing—how does one get from neural networks to the experience of me, here, now? If neural networks are conscious, why me, here, now rather than someone else, somewhere else, some other time? But no doubt the someone else could ask the same question. Sometimes I think that the question itself is based on a misunderstanding. It is like the question, 'Why am I here rather than somewhere else?' Perhaps those who do not understand the question are right not to understand it, and it is I who am confused.[80]

THE MYSTICAL WORLD

Is materialism the only possible rational description of the world?

I keep a niggling doubt that the paradigm through which I see and interpret the world is not the only possible valid one. The materialist world view is not recent, but its dominance is. Its dominance derives from the eighteenth century enlightenment, the work of natural scientists from that age, and the industrial revolution that followed. Although it turns out that the universe is not anything like as clockwork as Newton's model would imply, we are educated to see the world as a mechanism, albeit extraordinarily complex and

---

[80] An interesting critique of the idea that the universe arises out of consciousness is to be found at http://nirmukta.com/2009/12/14/biocentrism-demystified-a-response-to-deepak-chopra-and-robert-lanzas-notion-of-a-conscious-universe/

subtle. But does the success of scientific investigation in explaining the material world necessarily mean that the spiritual world disappears into atoms and molecules?

Put another way, does the success of material science in explaining physical phenomena give the materialist world view the authority to interpret religion, art, ethics and mystical states?

The unfolding of this question has been going on since the time of the Ancient Greeks. The world was once full of gods inhabiting universals, the arts, and particular places. I say 'inhabiting' rather than 'standing for' because the universe was understood as a living thing. Human beings were part of the divine order, an order in which concepts such as *arete* (virtue) and *dike* (justice) referred to active principles underlying the way things were, rather than being merely human constructs. The view of the world as a living whole in which God was intimately involved carried on through the Middle Ages.[81]

There are those who still argue for this more integrated view, and point to the looming catastrophe that has resulted from the separation of humans from nature. The Advaita (non-dualistic) Vedanta has it that 'You are in everything in the world and everything in the world is in you since it only exists because it is mirrored in you; and at the same time you are that—everything.'[82]

However that may be, I find it very hard to think my way out of the materialist paradigm in which I was educated.

It is easier to believe in a universal order when the world we inhabit is bigger than us and carries on irrespective of what we humans do. This of course is no longer the case, given that our activities are causing climate change and mass extinctions. We are on our own. We cannot assume that

---

[81] See, for example, Joseph Milne, *The Mystical Cosmos*, Temenos Academy Papers no.37, 2013

[82] Shankaracharya, quoted in Beckwith p.141

things will carry on much as before and we cannot depend on higher powers to solve our problems. We need to develop a new way of understanding the world, a new myth for living by, without abandoning reason.

What knowledge can we get from 'higher states'?

Knowledge from revelation is only useful if it can be backed up by reason and experience. That is why I have said little about Rodney Collin's contribution to the fourth way literature. Rodney Collin underwent a strange episode after Ouspensky's death[83] and reported being taught the secrets of the universe by Ouspensky some time later.[84]

Mystical experiences are of little help to anyone who hasn't had them. However it is not impossible that such experiences might be very important. The problem with such states is that they cannot be demonstrated intellectually or in the world as a normal physical experiment. So, for example, by using a psychologist's questionnaire one might show that transcendental meditation reduces stress, but if meditation led to a profound experience of cosmic reality, then the best one could do to communicate this would be in some art form. In order to work at all, such an art form would have to connect with something similar in the person experiencing the art form.

Verification would have to occur by replicating in oneself whatever got the mystic to what they experienced. This would be a valid approach but not shareable in the usual way of scientific demonstration.

It would be similar to going to (say) northern Norway and seeing the northern lights in the days when there were no cameras, then coming back and describing what one had seen. That is, the experience would perhaps not be believed

---

83 Collin-Smith pp.44-5

84 Rodney Collin, The Theory of Eternal Life, preface

by anyone who hadn't seen it, and the only way of verifying it would be to go to Norway.

It might be argued that the meaning of a mystical experience would still not be interpretable in terms of ordinary life. How would we reconcile a vision that everything is connected in love (*agape* in Christian vocabulary) and bliss (*ananda* in Vedanta) with a materialist understanding that we are mere specks, chance events in a vast impersonal universe? Could we live with both understandings at the same time?

It seems to me possible that we mortals could have access to a better state of mind than the one we usually inhabit. It is possible that the world we have constructed for ourselves is inimical to the tranquility and happiness that we could under other circumstances enjoy. Perhaps mystical states are merely tasters of what could be normal psychology. We wouldn't have to be immortal for this to be a good thing.

If so, this would be the birthright of everyone, and once schools of awakening had sufficient graduates, they could teach the rest. They would need to avoid building bizarre orthodoxies on the results of cosmic visions.

COSMIC CONSCIOUSNESS

'Cosmic consciousness' is not a fourth way term. Gurdjieff said that it means different things depending on who says it, and in some cases it is 'simply fantasy, associative daydreaming connected with intensified work of the emotional centre.'[85] In this section I use the term precisely because it is vague. It may or may not refer to fourth state.

What I wish to discuss are those states of higher or special consciousness which sometimes occur spontaneously, occasionally from drug experiences or for no obvious reason —states in which all our worries and preoccupations drop away and we experience a sense of the wonder or the unity of

---

[85] In *Search of the Miraculous* p.116

everything and a deep sense of peace. Perhaps as expressed in the Upanishads:

> That is perfect. That is perfect. Perfect comes from perfect. Take perfect from perfect, the remainder is perfect. May peace and peace and peace be everywhere.[86]

Maybe some have never experienced such a state, or have and have mostly forgotten it or discounted it, and yet others have made it the centre of their life's search. As mentioned in the section on SES, I had an ego-less state once as a result of transcendental meditation, but have not recovered exactly that state since, whether in meditation or otherwise. I have also had lesser states, a simple feeling of warmth radiating from the chest area accompanied by a feeling of general wellbeing and the suspension of worries, even though I knew that the state was temporary and that the usual anxieties would return.

It seems to me that falling in love is a related experience, in which the existence of the other transforms the vision, not only of she or he who is the object of that love, but also of everything else. Of course we can fall out of love too. Although it is a commonplace belief that love is blind, I have heard it claimed that when we are in this state of love we see things as they truly are, and it is when we descend into our usual state that we lose sight of reality. In the *Phaedrus* Plato has Socrates say:

> This then is the fourth type of madness, which befalls when a man, reminded by the sight of beauty on earth of the true beauty, grows his wings and endeavours to fly upwards.[87]

Such states can be translated by the mind into revelations about the nature of the universe. The feeling of the

---

[86] Shree Purohit Swami & W. B. Yeats, *The ten principal Upanishads*, Faber & Faber 1970, p.15

[87] Plato, *Phaedrus*, Jowett translation, 249

connectedness of everything, combined with the ego-loss that goes with it, suggests that this silent consciousness lies at the heart of everything. 'I' as a separate being simply do not exist in the way that 'I' normally imagine. It begins to make sense that everything evolves (in the sense of unfolding) and condenses from that central still point. From this perspective the idea of finer and coarser matters and the idea of the great illusion of the creation emerge: understanding that 'I' is an illusion extends to the idea of the illusion of everything else.

Attempts have been made to draw from such experiences an account of the nature of the universe. I have yet to find any that are convincing. Many are based on misunderstandings of scientific discoveries, particularly of quantum mechanics. Quantum entanglement, for example, while it suggests that everything is mysteriously connected, cannot enable the transfer of information instantaneously from one side of the universe to the other, despite what some claim.[88]

While it is perfectly right to be in awe of the extraordinary universe we live in, there is no currently respectable way of joining physics with mystical experiences, nor is there yet any meaningful way of showing how the material world could derive from consciousness, albeit it is also hard to show how consciousness could arise from matter.

It may be that the universe is simply material, not in the Gurdjieffian sense of finer matters interpenetrating coarse in a hierarchy of finer and finer substances, but in the sense that modern physics has demonstrated: fields existing on an inconceivably small scale, their behaviour described by

---

[88] For example, Beckwith p.245. Observing the spin state of an entangled electron tells us what the spin state of its pair is, but you can't know what the spin state of either particle was until you make your observation. Hence you have found out something but not transmitted anything.

mathematical relationships somehow leading to the world at our own scale in which things feel solid and familiar. If this vision is right then it is not that finer matters interpenetrate coarse, but that everything is made of the same something: abstract, mathematical, no less real just because we don't intuitively understand it. And just because we don't understand it this does not give us permission to make up stories about it or to believe whatever we like.

If we take this view then there is of course still room for mystical experiences, for cosmic consciousness, call it what you will (and very probably it is more than one thing). These experiences are facts, and facts are part of what science deals with. It is the job of science, not to arrive at a dogma or set of beliefs, but on the contrary to ask questions and devise tests to clarify what is a plausible theory and what is not.

There arises the question, then, about the nature of these states. If we are to stick strictly to what we know then we ought not to build religious or metaphysical doctrines on them. There is clearly potential value in states of being that promote inner peace and a condition in which ego is in abeyance, states which encourage seeing the unity in everything (since after all everything exists in relation to everything else). If this is the case, then there will be value in techniques which tend to produce such states, always assuming that the outcome is a more tolerant and co-operative world rather than a population of spaced-out lotus-eaters, or indeed a minority cult that separates itself from everyone else.

TIME

Ouspensky was preoccupied with the idea of recurrence even before meeting Gurdjieff. Recurrence is different from reincarnation. In this theory, everything repeats exactly and mechanically as before, and time is a circle. I think Ouspensky may have got the idea from Nietzsche, whose argument for recurrence was that if the universe is composed of a vast but finite number of material causes and effects, perhaps of atoms and molecules interacting like Newtonian billiard balls, eventually everything must come back into the same configuration again and thus repeat mechanically exactly as before.

We now know that this comes up against the laws of thermodynamics, according to which the entropy or disorder of a closed system always increases. Consider the act of throwing the contents of a box of matches out of the box. How likely is it that the matches will spontaneously jump back into the box? Taking the universe as a whole, the probability that not only the matches, but everything else will repeat exactly as before, is so vanishingly minute as to say that it is impossible. If somehow entropy were reversed, time would go backwards. Even if everything disappeared into a black hole, came out the other side and started all over again in exactly the same way, chaos theory shows that even tiny fluctuations can cause massive changes later on. In addition, randomness is aided by quantum effects. In short, Nietzsche was wrong.

Ouspensky thought that if we strive to awaken then this supposed mechanical repetition can be broken, and for those beginning to awaken one's time becomes a spiral instead of a circle.

To understand the chain of reasoning here, we have to assume that consciousness stands above and separate from the material world and is independent of its laws. If we imagine (despite all of the above) a Newtonian clockwork universe at some point arriving back at the same configuration of atoms as before, then what could interrupt this cycle of repetition except conscious work? That is, as long as consciousness is capable of re-setting the clockwork.

If we take the idea of recurrence at a much more local and psychological level then it makes a lot more sense. Our lives do have a certain repetitive quality, particularly noticeable when unfortunate events repeat themselves. We might for example leave a harmful relationship and shortly afterwards get into another one, or repeatedly make the same mistakes in job interviews, or fail to overcome social awkwardness, or lose weight and then put it back on again, or drink too much alcohol even though we regretted it last time. We acquire certain maladaptive patterns of behaviour which make our lives less happy than they might be.[89] We have recurring internal dialogues, perhaps of self-criticism or of over-compensatory vanity. This is an area where greater self-awareness and some courage could help us break out of the hamster-wheel.

TIME IS A FACTOR

As already recorded, in my youth I was for about four years a member of the SES, which despite some later controversy about the organisation, I look back on as being on the whole, for me, benign. It had overall a positive effect on me. However, as noted before, I got the impression from the

---

[89] Charles M. Schultz's cartoon character Charlie Brown appears in a recurring situation in which Lucy encourages him to kick a ball. He tells her that she will just whip the ball away at the last moment like last time, causing him to fall over. Lucy says that she will not do it this time. He runs to kick the ball and Lucy takes it away at the last moment, causing him to fall over. In the last frame Charlie Brown says, from a horizontal position, "When, when, when, when, when will I ever learn?"

early lectures that by practising certain simple exercises one could achieve enlightenment (or whatever they called it) within a reasonable time-frame. Part of my reason for leaving was that after four years I was much the same as I had been when I entered, albeit I knew a lot more about the Italian Renaissance and Baroque music than I had at the beginning.

Actually, to digress, part of the problem was that no spiritual tradition that I had come across addressed in any way the turmoil of youth in searching for a love interest or the difficult matter of sex. I was told, however, not to worry about it, because by working on oneself eventually these things would take care of themselves. Sure enough a few decades later this came true, but quite a lot of experience gradually and sometimes painfully acquired was involved in the process. (There is actually a shortcut, nothing to do with the fourth way, but this is not that book.)

To return to the matter in hand, the Fellowship got around the time problem by saying, 'time is a factor.' On the one hand, the present moment is always before you, on the other it takes years of effort to become a man or woman no. 5. Well, not so much years as lifetimes. The fact that none of us are 'conscious beings' yet is explained by the idea that it takes a lifetime of effort to ascend the spiritual staircase one rung. So we might become man or woman no. 5 in our next lifetime or several lifetimes hence.

It did not occur to me that this was a little at odds with Ouspensky referring to the fourth way as 'the way of the sly man,' and that this way is supposedly quicker than the other ways. 'The sly man will produce this state in the shortest time of all.'[90]

Robert Burton claimed that it takes nine lifetimes for 'ascending souls' to become conscious. I have no idea what evidence there is or could be for this. Latterly he would give some students 'eighth lifetime photographs.' Sometimes he

---

[90] Fourth Way p.98

would say at a dinner event, 'all of you are in your eighth lifetimes.' This is not standard fourth way teaching and it appears to be an invention of Mr Burton, albeit he claimed not to innovate.

It is interesting that spiritual teachers sometimes make ex-cathedra statements but don't explain how they know. It is good practice to ask for evidence. But no-one asked.

IMMORTALITY

> It's no use going back to yesterday, because I was a different person then.
> —Lewis Carroll[91]

> We are such stuff as dreams are made on, and our little life is rounded with a sleep.
> —Shakespeare[92]

The slowness of progress towards some exalted state of consciousness, then, is to be excused by the idea of multiple lifetimes. At the same time the idea of potential immortality is slipped in. A conscious being at the level of man no. 7, according to Ouspensky, becomes immortal at the scale of the solar system 'according to another description.'[93]

Immortality is problematic, partly because it doesn't solve any real problems and partly because the meaning of immortality is inadequately specified.

Immortality doesn't solve the problems of life

There is a paradox here, because during my time in the school the emphasis became more and more on being present, being in the moment. If I am present, what difference does it make whether I live forever or not?

---

[91] Lewis Carroll, *Alice's Adventures in Wonderland*, ch.10

[92] *The Tempest*, Act IV, scene 1

[93] *Psychology* p.46, *In Search of the Miraculous* pp.44, 215

As the philosopher Wittgenstein wrote, "The temporal immortality of the human soul, that is to say, its eternal survival after death, is not only in no way guaranteed, but this assumption in the first place will not do for us what we always tried to make it do. Is a riddle solved by the fact that I survive for ever?"[94]

The whole benefit of the work of being present is precisely living in the present moment. Past and future exist as theories only.

Wittgenstein continues: "Is this eternal life not as enigmatic as our present one? The solution of the riddle of life in space and time lies outside space and time."[95]

I don't think Wittgenstein was arguing at all for immortality. Rather, the problems we have in trying to live meaningful and happy lives are not solved by extending our lives indefinitely.

The concept of immortality is incompletely specified

The idea of immortality is problematic in any case. We change all the time, so what is it that survives death, assuming anything can? Personality is regarded by the fourth way as simply an artificial mask, to be used or discarded as occasion requires, so we should not expect personality to be reincarnated. In any case, it is something children acquire rather than are born with.

Shall memories lost through the passage of time (let alone through the depredations of dementia) be restored somehow? Who has memories of a past life? And if we are not reborn with our memories, then what is left?

Does our child-like essence somehow survive? If somehow our essence survives—a bunch of tendencies to act and

---

[94] Ludwig Wittgenstein, *Tractatus* 6.4312
[95] ibid.

perceive in particular ways together with some spark of consciousness—in what sense is what is reborn still 'us'?[96]

Is immortality extension in eternity?

Rodney Collin claimed that time is a spiral, and one's moments of being in the present, one's moments of real consciousness, light up like jewels on the spiral and in some way those real moments exist in eternity.[97] Eternity is perhaps a dimension other than time, in which things exist outside time. However my describing eternity as a dimension is poetical rather than anything that can stand intelligent scrutiny. Can we be extended in eternity? If so, how would we know? What would that actually mean? Would the direction of eternity, different from the spiral of time, continue when the spiral stopped? If we die in time do we continue to exist in eternity?

In the third state time does seem in some way to stand still. Yet everything still moves. Time is not abolished.

---

[96] Many years ago I saw a programme on television about past life regression. Some therapists reckoned that by hypnotism they could get their clients to remember past lives. A number of cases were presented including one where what was remembered was an historically obscure massacre of some Jews in York in the Middle Ages. This was very intriguing, because as presented the client was not an historian and allegedly knew nothing about the Medieval history of York. In another case a client remembered being a Roman soldier. I found it surprising that no-one thought of asking him anything in Latin. Surely if you can remember being a Roman soldier you ought to be able to remember your mother-tongue? Of course he might have been recruited from some other ethnic group. However one can be certain that his mother tongue would not have been English, since that language had yet to exist.

[97] The Theory of Celestial Influence p.339

Gurdjieff's view on immortality

In places Gurdjieff emphasises our mortality: "...every one of these unfortunates during the process of existence should constantly sense and be cognisant of the inevitability of his own death...," and "...even every 'complete victim' of contemporary education should understand without shuddering and know, that Hell and Paradise do indeed exist, but only not there 'in that world' but here beside us on Earth."[98]

He also said that "If there is anything in a man, it may survive; if there is nothing, then there is nothing to survive."[99] It may of course be pointed out that this only applies to the 'three-brained beings,' in other words, all of us who have not acquired permanent consciousness and will.[100] That is why the Work is urgent. But the System also tells us that very few of us will achieve this.

The justification for this in turn is that very few of us want to awaken in the first place. It is not unjust that few make it, because few choose it. But of those who choose it, how many achieve it?

We are in the same state as Ibsen's Peer Gynt, not wanting to be melted down with all the other buttons by the button-moulder, but at the same time not having even enough soul to be able to sell it to the devil.

For those of us who are puffs of wind, we still have the option of learning to be the best puffs of wind that we can. If we are not immortal, then we must return to the view of the ancients, that it is others' memory of us that we leave behind, and the results of what we have accomplished, for better or

---

[98] *Beelzebub* book 3, pp.373, 428

[99] In Search of the Miraculous p.32

[100] ibid. p.91

worse. In human cultural history the idea of immortality is relatively new.[101]

Most of these arguments occurred to me before I had formed the intention to leave the Fellowship. The last meeting I led at the London Centre was on the topic of eternity, and in it I put forward the idea that immortality and becoming man or woman no. 5 were both irrelevant to being in the present. If we are present now, what does it mean to be man or woman no. 5, since the whole point of being a higher being is to be present? Similarly, immortality is not now, it is some other time. In addition to the quotations from Wittgenstein given above I quoted this:

> If we take eternity to mean not infinite temporal duration but timelessness, then eternal life belongs to those who live in the present.[102]

---

[101] *The Epic of Gilgamesh*, to which Gurdjieff refers in *Meetings with Remarkable Men*, is the oldest known story. In it the hero, Gilgamesh, goes in search of immortality, which he fails to achieve.

[102] Wittgenstein, *Tractatus* 6.4311

DISQUIETING TALES

The school did not teach social skills.

During my time in the school I married twice. The first time was to my long-standing wife with whom I had already had two children, and we decided to formalise it. She was not a Fellowship member, and had put up with my frequent attendances at the Fellowship without her. We invited a group of the London students over for an informal reception at our house. They all gathered together and talked to each other, and no-one attempted to strike up conversation with any of my family members. I felt that it was not from deliberate rudeness but rather from simply having forgotten —or never having learned—how to interact with people outside the Fellowship. I probably made too many allowances for them as I am myself not good at small-talk, and it is a skill I have had to make an effort to acquire. But now I regard it as part of what the fourth way calls *external considering*. If it is true, as Robert Burton said more than once, that we are not better than anyone, just luckier than everyone, then there can be no justification for not making the effort to put people at their ease, to show an interest. In retrospect it was embarrassing.

Much later I married again to my present wife, who briefly joined the Fellowship. She was never accepted by them, despite other recently joined members becoming an integral part of the London Centre very quickly. At least one member behaved as though she thought my wife would take me away from the school, and I was warned 'not to lose what you have gained.' No-one made any serious attempt to befriend her, although one or two were reasonably courteous.

I can confidently assert that it was not my wife who took me away, but a dawning awareness that the school and the Teacher had run out of ideas, of impetus, that it had become anaemic and was what is called in the Work language, *a descending octave.*

Another incident sticks in my mind. During the glory days of the London Centre when I happened to be Centre Director we had more than one visit from Robert, and among other events we organised teaching dinners, which required a musician to play at the beginning. We had no accomplished musicians among the London students and it was my job to source them, usually professional harpists, who would be paid. One time none of my contacts were available and I asked my teenage daughter if she would play cello, as by that time she was playing at a near-professional standard. She agreed but it was my mistake that no payment was negotiated —she was doing me a favour. She played very well. Afterwards Robert made no attempt to thank her or even speak to her. I feel bad now that I did not at least insist on payment from the London Centre.

How the Teacher treated his own

One incident sticks in my mind. Again, I wish only to report what I myself witnessed.

On one visit to Apollo I stayed in the home of a charming elderly couple, both devoted members of the Fellowship living near the property. The lady of the house, G., later developed a medical condition that resulted in some problem with eating. When I visited Apollo on a subsequent occasion I was told that Robert had asked that G. not attend teaching dinners, because of the impression her disorder would cause.

I was surprised at this, because to my mind this would have been good work of *external consideration* for the other students who would attend. Thinking of this now, I am reminded that Robert frequently said, "This is a school of love." To my present shame, I 'buffered' the contradiction.

RUMOURS

I said at the beginning that I would only report what I know. But this can hardly be complete without at least alluding to a few things I heard.

Once I was dining with friends at their house near the property, and they had invited friends of theirs to join us. During the meal this couple talked about their disturbance at Robert's sexual behaviour. I remember, not exactly defending it, but saying that in my understanding one would pay a very high price to get the knowledge of awakening, and if that meant sleeping with the Teacher then that was a price that some would pay. My current understanding is very different. I understand that using a position of power to get sexual favours (or any other kinds of favour) is abusive, and to those involved, damaging. I do not think my argument convinced them, as it was not long after that that they both left the school. I was, back then, part of the problem, as indeed is anyone who remains once certain facts are made clear to them.

It can always be said that those who had sexual relations with the Teacher did so voluntarily. But when there is a power imbalance the onus is on the one with the power to consider the welfare of others especially carefully.

I also heard a student complain to others in my hearing that Robert had stolen her boyfriend: not in this case that he had had sexual relations with him but that he had advised the student's boyfriend to cease the relationship and take up with another. When things like this are heard at second hand it is always possible to rationalise them: friends do sometimes advise friends that a particular relationship is not good for them. Was this friendly advice or was it the arbitrary exercise of power? I also heard an allegation from another that Robert had stolen her husband in a more direct way. Again, I report what I heard but have nothing to back it up: it is hearsay. Unfortunately there are a lot of these stories. But at second-hand I cannot make definitive statements, and while a member, the exercise against gossip together with the exercise of not socialising with ex-students shuts down any further discussion.

If one is to believe the tales on the notorious blog,[103] abuse was persistent and extensive, starting well before I joined and continuing. But disturbing stories I actually heard were few and quickly forgotten. Once when I was visiting Apollo a student who had recently left staged a protest outside the gateway to the property. Some students would stop and talk to her, but very quickly Robert made it a task, a requirement not to talk to her. This was followed rapidly by a Court Order restraining her from being in the vicinity of the property.

One more episode sticks in my mind, although this is second-hand information. Robert requested that students not play jazz. Classical music was allowed as was folk music, and somewhat arbitrarily Motown was permitted as well. Nevertheless some students at Apollo had a club at which jazz was played. At one of these events a student had a sub-arachnoid haemorrhage (a kind of stroke). Robert interpreted this as a message from Influence C that jazz was not wanted on the Ark. It seems that all manner of suffering is acceptable from 'higher forces' because when we 'complete our roles,' having learned whatever we are supposed to learn, we shall go on to our next life. This is one of the dangers of the belief in multiple lifetimes: a callous disregard for suffering in the present.

---

[103] https://robertearlburton.blogspot.com/

TEACHERS OF SPIRITUALITY

THE CIRCLE OF ILLUSION

A circle of illusion is any closed system of thought. It is a system in which there is an answer from within the system, justifying the system, to any possible question.

If you disagree with the Teacher it is not because the Teacher is wrong but because you have too much self-will. If anything either good or bad happens to you it is Influence C teaching you something. People leave the School not because it no longer has anything useful to give them, but because they turn their backs on Influence C. This is a problem with any truth from revelation or from established tradition: it is self-validating and therefore cannot be questioned (the philosopher Karl Popper levelled the same accusation against psychoanalysis: if you disagree with the analyst your analysis clearly is not complete).

In addition, systems of thought that are not theoretically closed can suffer from confirmation bias. Anything that tends to confirm our beliefs is accepted uncritically, and anything that tends to disconfirm our beliefs is ignored or explained away. This was seen for example in the absurd politicisation of hydroxychloroquine (HCQ) for the treatment of covid-19. Because this treatment was touted by President Trump as effective, doctors who happened to be in favour of President Trump kept backing HCQ even as evidence of its ineffectiveness accumulated. 'It's because they're using it on seriously ill people and it should be used early in the disease.' 'It's because they didn't combine it with zinc.' And so on. In a similar way, the failure of Robert Burton's predictions was explained by him as Influence C intentionally creating humility in him, rather than that Influence C were a figment of his imagination as were the predictions.

LIMITS TO FOLLOWING A TEACHER

> *May be the devil, and the devil hath power*
> *T' assume a pleasing shape. Yea, and perhaps*
> *Out of my weakness and my melancholy,*
> *As he is very potent with such spirits,*
> *Abuses me to damn me. I'll have grounds*
> *More relative than this.*
> —Shakespeare, *Hamlet* Act 2 scene 2

The main danger of spiritual schools is probably the immunity of the teacher or guru to criticism. The problem with a guru who is supposedly on a much higher plane than the rest of us is that he or she is supposedly subject to higher laws and therefore his or her behaviour, no matter how questionable from the point of view of ordinary morality, can always be explained away as in some way for our benefit.

The teacher makes the rules and "You must understand that all rules are for self-remembering."[104]

In *Notes on the Decision to Work*, Ouspensky writes: "Understanding of the necessity for obeying rules and direct instructions must be based on the realisation of your mechanicalness and your helplessness.

"Think very seriously: are you really ready and willing to obey, and do you fully understand the necessity for it? There is no going back. If you agree and then go back, you will lose everything that you have acquired up to that time, and you will lose more really, because all that you acquired will turn into something wrong in you. There is no remedy against this."[105]

These considerations create the perfect situation in which corruption of a teacher and the duping of students can occur. You either do whatever the teacher requires or you become food for the moon.

---

[104] Psychology p.97

[105] Conscience pp.137-140

A teacher is naturally presumed to know more than the student. However in a normal teaching situation the student can question the teacher and if the teacher is any good, questions can be answered in language the student can understand.

It may be that the Fellowship is unusually pathological in this respect. "Schools are not intended to make sense," a saying in the Fellowship, was particularly relevant when the unpreparedness of the school for the various predicted disasters was so manifest. Far from stockpiling canned goods and preparing a nuclear bunker, camels were imported, as well as a startling collection of Rococo ornaments. The teacher was turning into a kind of latter-day Roi Soleil. I used vaguely to assume that somehow or other everything was being guided by higher forces and the purpose of this apparent insanity would become clear when the time came.

Nevertheless, Ouspensky left his own teacher, Gurdjieff. "In regard to my relations with G. I saw clearly at this time that I had been mistaken about many things that I had ascribed to G. And that by staying with him now I should not be going in the same direction I went at the beginning."[106]

THE POWER OF A TEACHER

What I tell you three times is true
—Lewis Carroll, The Hunting of the Snark

That a spiritual teacher can have a powerful and charismatic effect is clear. What is behind it is less clear, and could be due to a number of different causes.

Perhaps some are looking for a path to follow in a confusing world, as I was, and a way out of a mild chronic depression, as also I was, although I would not have expressed it in that way. Perhaps some are looking for a father figure, a guide who takes away all fears. Perhaps some

---

[106] In Search of the Miraculous p.374

are looking for missing love. We are all capable of projecting our ideal onto someone who seems to fit that ideal closely enough.

We also all crave certainty. At the time I left the Fellowship, Donald Trump was President of the United States, and whenever I heard on the television or radio his statements on a whole range of matters I was instantly reminded of Robert Burton. This was not me being cynically clever, the feeling came in before I had analysed it. At first I thought it was because of the slightly breathy voice, and that was probably part of it. But then I realised that what they have in common is the habit of uttering statements without any attempt at producing evidence. They act as though a thing were true merely because they have said it.

Always ask for evidence. And remember that *extraordinary claims require extraordinary evidence.* I have often been told, 'Science doesn't know everything,' as though that were sufficient excuse to believe more or less any improbable claim. The magic and charm of the claim is taken as sufficient proof. There is not time to investigate everything, and there is no shame in politely disdaining to look for evidence for someone else's un-evidenced proposition. That is not having a closed mind as long as one is open to new evidence once it is produced.

In matters of practical skill the evidence has to come from one's own efforts. If you practice calligraphy enough you will eventually be able to write beautifully. If you practice archery you will eventually be able to hit the bulls-eye. There are techniques that have worked for others before you and you can apply them. And it is true that anyone who wants to learn something is usually better off finding a teacher. The caveat is that a good teacher manages to teach you something, and when you have learned it you go and do it. You graduate. A teacher you have to stick to for life is arguably not doing the job properly.

How to verify a teacher

It is quite possible that there could be spiritual schools that are not corrupt, but I think that if you accept anyone as your spiritual teacher whose word on spiritual matters (or any other matters) is treated as infallibly true, then corruption, at least of the teacher, is highly likely to result.

We may take it from what has gone before that men and women no.s 6 and 7 are highly theoretical. A man no. 7 is said to have crystallised higher intellectual centre as well as higher emotional centre. Robert Burton claims to be a man no. 7 (or 8—I've lost count). The teacher in the SES (the Shankaracharya) was claimed to be 'a fully-realised man.'

The fourth way teaches that the lower cannot see the higher, which relates also to the fact that we cannot imagine what waking is really like when we are dreaming. Therefore if someone comes along and claims to be any level of human being above no. 4 (or 1, 2 and 3, given that men and women no. 4 only really exist as aspirants to higher consciousness) there is no obvious way of testing this.

This opens the question as to how a seeker after esoteric knowledge (assuming such knowledge exists) is to assess professed teachers of such knowledge.

A simple procedure for assessing a teacher in anything is to ask the question, does this person know more about the subject than I do? And in the case of an applied art, which practical esoteric work aspires to be (both SES and the Fellowship call themselves 'practical' schools), does this person manifest in ways which I should like to be able to emulate?

Another method would be to look at the number and quality of the graduates. Regrettably the Fellowship has none.

Mere knowledge of spiritual matters is no guarantee of anything. A person can know Bible passages by heart or offer supposed interpretations of the Bhagavad Gita and still be a scoundrel or self-deceived.

Certainly indulging in unkind or selfish behaviour would disqualify, if we follow Ouspensky's claim that conscience is essential.[107] Some doubtful behaviour might be explained away as for the student's spiritual benefit, like the whacks given to students in some Zen koans (and in any case the monks probably knew what they were signing up for). However a pattern of repeated disregard for others' welfare should set off alarm bells. Thus while we may not be able to verify that a teacher is genuine, we may be able to falsify the claim.

Do schools of awakening help the world?

There was a fundamental difference between the SES as I experienced it and the Fellowship, in relation to the intention towards the world outside the organisation.

When I was in the youth group of SES there was the feeling that the activity of the school might be of benefit to the world. One youth group member was studying for the Church of England priesthood, and Mr N, the youth group leader, speculated how that student could become a beacon of light if he became Archbishop of Canterbury.

SES was where I also heard the idea that universities are the leaven of society. It is not necessary or desirable that all courses of study feed directly into economic production. The world of the mind and the arts are also important.

It was during my time in the youth group that we first put on a public event at Waterperry. This was essentially a fete with a choir. We had been trained to sing Mozart's *Beatus* Vir and I think we sang at the fete. There was also a stall in which one could bowl in order to win a ham, and a local villager kept entering it until he won. This event gradually morphed into what later became *Art in Action*, an annual exhibition of the arts from all over the world, to which tens of thousands came.

---

[107] *Conscience* p.53

It is worth mentioning that the Maharishi believed that if only one percent of the world's population would practice Transcendental Meditation then there would be world peace. Even though I no longer practice TM I find this oddly plausible.

The desire to improve the world by inner transformation, one-by-one, was a big part of my joining the Fellowship. Not long after I joined I became aware that Robert's vision was creating an 'Ark' to survive nuclear war. On the one hand I did not find the idea that humanity would bring nuclear catastrophe on itself in the least surprising. The idea haunted me. On the other, this should have given me pause for thought, in that the aim of saving only a portion of humanity is radically different from the aim of doing something to improve life on earth for everyone. Nevertheless I persisted in the thought that inner transformation would be at least one small step to making the world a kinder place. Looking back, I was both right and wrong. I am still on a journey to be the best kind of human being I can be, and it is a daily struggle not without many failures. The Fellowship, however, is a very insular organisation and its leader cares nothing for those who are not touched by Influence C, and being touched by Influence C is more-or-less the same thing as making regular teaching payments.[108]

It may be that there is something worth learning from bits of the fourth way and systems like it, and it may be that only in the company of like-minded people can we learn it. But if you choose to try this, go in with an open mind but review the situation, preferably with an impartial non-member friend, from time to time and frequently.

This means that you will have to avoid any organisation that forbids discussion with outsiders, or else disobey the

---

[108] Robert Burton said that 'Higher Centres are designed to serve humanity.' *Self Remembering* p.138. However we must judge an organisation not by what it says but by what it does.

injunction. It is noteworthy that in The Study Society founded by Ouspensky's student Dr Roles, members were enjoined not to discuss the material with non-members or even students of other branches of the Ouspensky work.[109] In a similar way Fellowship members are forbidden from contact with ex-members.

Be clear about why you are attending, and consider writing down your aims at the beginning and review your aims from time to time, also in writing. This may help to prevent a drift in which you end up doing something entirely at odds with your original intention (see Law of Seven above).

In the preceding I have for the most part not given the SES a bad press. However I was only a member for four years and that was a long time ago. Keep your eyes open, your emotions alert and your analytical intellect asking questions, not just at the beginning but regularly. Verification, like being present, is a continuous process.

[109] Joyce Collin-Smith pp.48-9

ABANDONING THE SYSTEM

WHY DID I STAY?

Robert Burton said on more than one occasion that the way coyotes attack a house is that they lure the dog guarding the house into the open where they then surround and overcome him. The idea is that one may be lured away from the Work by 'life.'

On the one hand it makes sense to keep the company of those who share one's aim. It makes sense to be with people who will see through our acts and our false personality and gently correct us. If we want to live closer to essence, then this is useful.

On the other hand the work takes place in ordinary life. If what we learn is genuine and true then it can endure difficulty and stand up to criticism. Discussing the work of the School with non-members would lead to exposing the ideas of the School to critical appraisal. While I am happy to defend what I have verified, or indeed remain silent but confident in what I know, having some of the ideas open to scrutiny would expose the fact that they are mere beliefs, unfounded on anything other than the Teacher's say-so.

In this I am as guilty as anyone. Yet it seemed reasonable to me only to discuss with non-members what they wanted to know, and even then I would usually only be interested in discussing what seemed to me then the core ideas, the things I found useful. Because of this I did not have to speak of the crazier beliefs of Robert's teaching: the forty-four conscious beings supposedly guiding our School and that Robert is personally guided by Leonardo da Vinci. In my early enthusiasm I did once mention something of this to a friend not in the School and he had the tact not to question it—and I realised for that moment that I had said something that sounded absurd.

During much of my time in the School I had a fear of losing the School. I might perhaps be tempted to leave because of the monetary payments, or for some other reason unspecified. This fear was because I had lost a School already (SES), had ceased meditating and had forgotten even the exercise of pausing between activities. It was a shock to remember that there were exercises that could be used to come into the moment and to be present to what one was doing, and that I had made no deliberate efforts of that kind for nineteen years. I had once had a quest and I had forgotten it. That I had been reminded of it felt like being chosen, being given a second chance. I came to believe that second chances are rare and third chances probably non-existent.

Although at the time of joining the School I had no concept of Influence C as being the ghosts of conscious beings, I came to believe that if I lost the School that would be the end of my hopes for conscious evolution. I did not think about becoming 'food for the moon,' because although I did not reject the idea, neither did it make any sense to me. Robert refers to students who leave as having lost Influence C, and that idea was closer to my fear. I comforted myself with the thought that my very fear was a sign that I was unlikely to lose the School.

QUESTIONS I SHOULD HAVE ASKED

A friend of mine left the school a few years ago. I asked him why. He said that he felt that we should have been told before we joined that the teacher was homosexual. I have to say that the sexual orientation of the teacher was not a concern of mine, and I felt it was irrelevant. I asked my friend, "The question is, did you get what you came for?" It seemed to me that opinions about the teacher's sexual activities were irrelevant.

What, however, should have caused me to pause was that the teacher surrounded himself with an entourage of young men, mostly of Russian extraction. I supposed that they were all there of their own will, and that perhaps the lifestyle they were able to enjoy in the West was superior to what they were used to in Russia. It did not occur to me to ask, what if they want to leave? Russia is not known for its tolerance of homosexuality, and I doubt whether all or even most of them were gay. And what careers could they look forward to if they left the organisation, which might have resulted in their deportation, since they were probably there on religious visas? There exists a blog in which ex-members make some pretty serious accusations, however it is an exercise in the school not to read it, and almost everyone does what they are told. As far as I was concerned, I had no wish to read other people's moans. However I also did not know what those moans were actually about.

Another feature of the Fellowship is the exercise of not talking to former members. This supposedly arises from the idea that payment is a principle. Those who left the school would think that they were getting something when in fact they were getting nothing, because supposedly the only way they could advance would be to re-join the school. So not talking to them was doing them a favour. Of course this also means remaining members do not hear the views of those who have left.

There was also an exercise not to indulge in gossip. On the face of it this was a reasonable exercise, since gossip tends to cause conversation to descend into unpleasantness and is usually mean and destructive. It is generally accepted in polite society that you do not say bad things about a person unless they are present to answer to what they are accused of. However this meant that hardly anyone ever discussed questions bearing on the morality of the teacher.

On a few legendary occasions there were rebellions when someone would speak out at a meeting. I only heard about these second-hand. The person concerned together with others of like mind would then leave the school or be expelled, which meant that unless you were there you never heard the detail.

Most people in the school, and certainly almost all new members, would not be aware of any controversy, or would believe that those who left would inevitably criticise. And looking at what is published by the school on the web, there is little to object to and some beautiful quotations which immediately appeal to the emotions. I am reminded of Jesus' reference to 'whited sepulchres.'[110]

'LIFE'

Eternity is in love with the productions of time.
—William Blake

Life is the term used by the School to refer to people not in the School. Strangely, for a term with such a positive meaning, in the School it has rather negative associations. Life people are those who live mechanically. We strivers after consciousness versus the unconscious, the walking sleepers. Us versus 'life' family, 'life' friends, everyone else.

Is the Fellowship a fourth way School? By that I mean, a school that takes place in everyday life. The answer has to be 'no.' Clearly Apollo is a kind of monastery, although many students have jobs outside the property, in Marysville, Sacramento and elsewhere. Others, those on salary, are tied to the property by their low-paid jobs working for the Fellowship itself. Entertaining non-student family and friends is not permitted on the property, and in any case the remoteness of Apollo makes contact with anyone outside difficult. It takes about six hours to drive from San Francisco airport to Apollo, and there is no other way than driving of getting there.

As for the centres around the world, necessarily students have ordinary jobs. However contact with 'life' family is discouraged. There is very much a 'them and us' mentality. To me this is a dereliction of the idea, not only that the work

---

[110] Matthew 23:27

takes place in life, but also of the idea of *good householder*. *Good householder* means not only taking care of one's personal appearance and paying bills on time but also emotional good householder: not neglecting friends and family.

WHY I LEFT—MESSAGE TO THE CENTRE DIRECTORS

This was the first draft of my message to the Centre Directors informing them of my intention to leave the School. In the final draft I omitted paragraphs nine to eleven referring to the failure of Robert's 2018 prediction and to his alleged behaviour, because I felt, and was advised by friends, that those who read it would be less likely to absorb the other points made.

When I was about seventeen years old I came across the fourth way ideas and joined a School (the School of Economic Science, not FoF). I remember it as a bright time, like a jewel in my life. Because of various youthful confusions, after four years I left. Some nineteen years later I had a very clear moment of self-remembering which came apparently out of nowhere, and at that moment I decided I must find again the people who know about this. I found an out-of-date bookmark in one of my books and spent some time phoning around the world until I contacted the FoF. I joined in London.

Like many I made efforts to self-remember, not to express negative emotions, not to inner-consider, to externally consider others, and to work with whatever exercises were prescribed to interrupt mechanicality and to promote awareness. I verified that I was in a state of waking sleep much of the time. I began to become free of a crippling inner-considering, to become more aware of my surroundings, to become more free of my reactions to other people's negativity, and to, as it were, walk upright as a human being.

At the same time other ideas were introduced, such as the food diagram, the ray of creation, higher hydrogens, body types and Influence C. There is no immediately obvious way to verify some of these ideas. I recall in my early days in the school it was not uncommon for someone to say something like, 'I'm not working with that idea at the moment,' meaning for example that they hadn't verified Influence C as taught in the school. As time has moved on, self-remembering is much less often mentioned, whereas other ideas, such as influence C, are mentioned frequently as though everyone in the school believes that Influence C exists in the form of 44 angels. The honest phrase 'I'm not working with that' is seldom if ever heard. To some extent, perhaps to a large extent, honest uncertainty became replaced by belief. I do not exempt myself from that.

The natural tendency of the mind to see patterns even where there are none means that it is very easy to 'verify' whatever it is one wants to believe, by seeing numbers and signs in random events. There has been a gradual transition from an environment of open questioning and experimentation to one of unquestioning belief in whatever Robert says.

In recent years Robert has talked less and less about self-remembering, a topic he once said he never tired of. He talks more and more about signs in art and omens in number plates and such. Whether or not these signs are genuine communications from past or present conscious beings, for myself I began to find the content of Robert's meetings less emotional. I found it hard to believe that, for example, the square trouser-leg in Diego Rivera's painting indicated that Diego Rivera was giving a message about four wordless breaths.

It is true, as Shakespeare says, that one can find 'tongues in trees, books in the running brooks, sermons in stones, and good in everything' (As You Like It). For me, that describes a clearer state of consciousness, but it does not depend on the strained interpretation of omens.

Nevertheless for some years I have given Robert the benefit of the doubt. If he is a conscious being then maybe he sees what I do not. That depends of course on the assumption that Robert is at a higher level of development than the rest of us. As a long-time member of the London Centre and an infrequent visitor to Apollo I can only judge by the quality of the students I see around me locally, and for the most part I see serious seekers making efforts. Also the benefits I have surely gained from being in the school went some way towards verifying the school as genuine, and by implication its founder.

Even so, my view of Robert was strained by his recent claim (2018) to have been visited by the Absolute. Mr Ouspensky somewhere says that in order for the Absolute to communicate directly with us, all the intervening worlds would have to be destroyed. This is quite different from any of us becoming aware of the 'still small voice' within. It is of course quite possible that Mr Ouspensky is wrong about this. But if we start to question Mr Ouspensky then we must of course question the whole fourth way edifice upon which our school is built. In the last analysis, nothing is verified except what we ourselves, through our own work, verify. This claim of Robert's to have been visited by the Absolute is what has finally broken my connection with the school.

[Omitted paragraphs]

Thus I was not in the least surprised when California did not fall into the sea on 21 October [2018], an event in any case highly improbable from what is known of plate tectonics. What we should be surprised about is that Robert did not want to warn the world of this impending catastrophe. Perhaps he himself did not believe the prediction? In any event, have we forgotten the idea of external consideration, once much talked about as a form of self-remembering in the emotional centre?

In the London Centre it is generally frowned upon to talk about 'life people' as though non-members were some inferior species, and Robert himself has said that we are not better than 'life,' just luckier. Yet it looks as though some took the impending drowning of millions as though it were something of little concern, other than in relation to securing the water supply at Apollo.

Something else needs to be mentioned, that is, the elephant in the room. No-one talks about Robert's behaviour, the kind of behaviour that might lead one to question whether he is a conscious being. We are asked as an exercise not to indulge in gossip, and as an exercise this is generally sound, as most gossip diminishes us. There has also been a task not to read the notorious blog. I have not read it since its inception, when it started with an account of an introductory meeting in London at which I was present (the description of events was like a parody of what had actually taken place—a warm-hearted door greeter was experienced as a 'heavy' by the writer, for example) and I saw no reason to read any more. Having read some of the blog recently I was severely shocked. I recognise that I have buffered along the way a number of clues that should have prompted further enquiry. I shall not repeat the many allegations that are out there on the web and easy to find.

[Submitted text resumes]

Putting all this together, it seems to me that the school is an octave supported largely by its students and to some extent irrespective of its leader. Whether there is a do-re-mi in a work octave I have yet to verify, but we have all experienced the intervals in which, if we do not put in intentional work, the octave bends and the direction changes unnoticed towards results unintended. I leave grateful for what I have gained from the Work ideas and from fellow students, but the School is going in a direction which I do not wish to follow.

I recommend to anyone reading this to reconnect with the fundamental, verifiable methods of the fourth way, which are self-remembering, external consideration and the non-expression and transformation of negative emotions. I can affirm that efforts to be present, to remember oneself, to externally consider, to transform negative emotions as best one can, are worthwhile efforts.

I would add, if the aim to be present has value, then the idea that one may one day become crystallised as a conscious being is immaterial, just as the idea of life after death is immaterial. What may become of us as future 'conscious beings' is largely imagination and a distraction from whatever simple task is in front of us right now.

The present is real. If there is a God, He can only be found in the present. There is a 'still small voice:' we can learn to hear it.

The mind-forged manacles[111]

Putting it all together, how did I end up believing six impossible things before breakfast?

First of all, many of the ideas in the fourth way depend on notions that are commonplace and generally unchallenged by probably the majority of people in the world—notions that nevertheless I have questioned in what I have written here. That consciousness is different in principle from ordinary matter and cannot be explained by it is held by many, and this, as I acknowledge, is at present an unsolved riddle. That there is an immaterial soul distinct from the body is a common belief across many cultures and goes back at least to the Ancient Egyptians. The idea of potential immortality is related.

Next, interest in altered states of consciousness, while not mainstream, is certainly widespread across cultures and in history. It is natural, even if of questionable validity, to take insights from altered states as giving insight into reality. Chuang Tzu famously said that he dreamed he was a butterfly and on waking wasn't sure whether he had been a man dreaming he was a butterfly or whether he was a butterfly dreaming he was a man. So when I experienced a state of momentary inner peace as a teenager, or later, wordless inner peace during meditation, I took that to be a taste of the true nature of the world, the bliss that is at the centre of everything. This is an idea present in the Upanishads as well as being expressed in these lines from the beautiful Quaker hymn that is also sung in the Church of England:

Drop Thy still dews of quietness,
Till all our strivings cease;
Take from our souls the strain and stress,

---

[111] phrase from William Blake's poem, London

And let our ordered lives confess
The beauty of Thy peace.

Breathe through the heats of our desire
Thy coolness and Thy balm;
Let sense be dumb, let flesh retire;
Speak through the earthquake, wind, and fire,
O still, small voice of calm.[112]

There must be few people who do not lack something, and some of us seek it in spiritual practices that promise something to fill a void, or redemption from what torments us. In my case, in retrospect I was lacking in love as a teenager and in self-confidence for most of my adult life. I now think that to arrive at inner peace ought not to require the adoption of a belief system of baroque complexity.

Next comes the obvious gain of belonging, and a new friendship group. Even shy people like me are social animals. Then add the insidious effect of believing one is somehow special and being in possession of special knowledge. (Thanks to this book you now have all that special knowledge, for much less than it cost me.)

Once in the cult, accepting the various exercises to 'interrupt mechanicality' and 'promote awakening' were part of the deal. That's what I was paying for. The effort to be present and drop the concerns of the moment is common sense and it works. In hindsight one could say that I did not need to spend twelve percent of my post-tax income to achieve that. But if something works, it is not unreasonable to expect that there is more where that came from: the promise of higher states of consciousness.

I then worked with other exercises as they came along. The student tipped by Robert Burton to become the next man no. 5 (but later sidelined) took the view that you accept

---

[112] John Greenleaf Whittier, adapted by Garrett Horder as the hymn, *Dear Lord and Father of Mankind*

exercises as an experiment. If you question why, then you are refusing the experiment instead of doing it and will gain nothing from it. The necessity for obedience is also emphasised in Ouspensky's *Notes on the Decision to Work*. This means that tasks given in the Fellowship, such as not communicating with former students and not reading the blog, were accepted as for our own good, whether we understood the reasons or not. But asking your music teacher why you have to practice scales doesn't stop you from practicing them, and doing the exercises ought not to have precluded asking why.

This remains a fundamental problem with any manifestation of the fourth way, because on the one hand both Ouspensky and Gurdjieff insisted on "the necessity for obeying rules and direct instructions,"[113] and on the other, Ouspensky left Gurdjieff according to one account because Gurdjieff abandoned verification in favour of belief.[114]

In some areas I retained my skepticism, where it did not clash with Fellowship teaching. I thought that the belief of so many at Apollo in alternative (that is to say, un-evidenced) medicine was partly due to an incomplete scientific education and partly due to the fact that proper medical care in the USA is unaffordable. Those students 'on salary' were on very low wages and almost certainly did not have medical insurance as part of the package.

Robert Burton was careful not to take sides in areas which did not interfere with his authority. On one occasion when he was visiting London I was asked to attend one of his entourage of young men who were staying with him at a West End hotel. I duly assessed the problem, which involved

---

[113] *Conscience* pp.137-140

[114] Ouspensky, *A Record of Meetings*, 9 October 1935. "In 1918 I parted with G. because something changed. He changed the first principles and demanded that people must believe, and must do what he tells them even if they don't understand."

a small wound on the young man's foot, advised and prescribed. While I was making my assessment one of the other young men started to enthuse about some unorthodox treatment. As I looked up with what was probably a Mr Spock-like indication of mild surprise, Robert, addressing the alternative medicine enthusiast, said, 'I think he knows more about it than you do, dear.'

A feature of the Fellowship and I assume of all cults is the cutting off of members from outside influences. The most insidious way this was accomplished was the idea that we had special or esoteric knowledge that had to be worked for, and therefore could not be readily appreciated by those not in the Work. We were encouraged only to share with outsiders what they specifically asked for. Thus hardly anyone shared the ideas with non-members. Contact with non-members was not encouraged, nevertheless in my case I had a non-Fellowship family and I simply did not discuss the ideas with them, partly because they were not interested. We were sealed internally, even while holding down ordinary jobs and living with non-members.

I have mentioned also the fear of 'losing Influence C.' If you believe, as I did, that meeting a school is rare, then 'losing Influence C' is the ultimate disaster, it is to lose one's only chance of awakening.

There are others for whom leaving the cult is more difficult than it was for me. Those on salary at Apollo may have few marketable skills and probably no savings. Their whole network of human relationships is at Apollo, particularly if they have cut themselves off from their 'life' families. Even those not at Apollo may have isolated themselves from non-members.

Is there more to it than that? Trying to fill a void in one's life, to find inner peace, being promised 'awakening' and 'higher states,' being given the feeling that one is special, specially chosen by Influence C, gaining a friendship group that validates one, being given ideas of subtly increasing absurdity that build on things one already believes, isolation from 'life' people who might challenge the ideas, the subtle discouragement of independent thought through peer-pressure, the fear of losing all one's possibilities.

Having left and then read the blog I am caught between believing I was a victim (by having been relieved of a lot of money) and believing I was an enabler (by helping to fund corruption). I feel a bit like some criminal who has been caught doing something obviously stupid, who says to the judge, 'It seemed like a good idea at the time, Your Honour.'

We are all in difficulty as far as belief is concerned. I came across a blog by an ex-member of the Fellowship who had also been sucked into other mind-controlling situations. He had become so averse to having his mind controlled that he claimed, in a blog post discussing mind control, that the reaction of governments world-wide to the covid-19 pandemic was itself a massive mind-control conspiracy. He quoted various statistics and other evidence to back this up. (The post was dated April 2020 and there are no subsequent posts retracting this claim.) We may, if we are not careful, jump from one absurdity to another. We wish to believe something and then collect evidence to back up what we believe.

Questioning everything carries the danger that we reject all conventional wisdom and fall into error by over-valuing our own cleverness, leaving us vulnerable to the next mistaken idea. It is possible that if you keep too open a mind, someone will throw some rubbish into it.

WHY THE MAGIC STOPPED WORKING

Looking back, my leaving was both gradual and sudden.

As mentioned at the beginning, the printed versions of Robert's meetings ceased to interest me some years before I left. I subscribed to the transcripts intermittently out of a sense of loyalty, but didn't even read most of them. I told myself that the School was progressing, away from an intellectual way of working and towards living the teaching, in which words were increasingly redundant. The Work didn't have to appeal to my intellectual centre. Odd, then, that such words as there were lacked any emotion or even much content. The ideas of Gurdjieff and Ouspensky were replaced by Robert's belief that every possible artefact from the past contained the numbers six and four: the four wordless breaths that are supposed to follow the inner recital of the six words of the Sequence.

Nearer the time of my leaving, Robert's meetings were relayed by video from Apollo and there would be a meeting at the London Teaching House to watch. I felt no desire to attend these either.

At some point during my last year, when still a committed member, I led a meeting on the topic of 'eternity.' I included some of the ideas that are in this book on the topic of immortality, in particular the irrelevance of imagining becoming men or women no. 5, and I used the Wittgenstein quotation that immortality doesn't solve any problems for us. Ironically it was Robert's increasing focus on being present that led me to see that the doctrine of nine lifetimes was entirely beside the point.

A member of the London Centre was asked to collect money towards 'impressions' for Apollo, to commemorate students who had recently died ('completed their role'). Usually Robert would have these things bought first and ask for money for them afterwards. In this case it was a pair of gilded candelabras, no doubt in the rococo style. I could not for the life of me see how buying candelabras would memorialise students who had died, as no-one was going to engrave names on antiques. Still a faithful member, I declined to contribute, even though some years previously I had contributed generously towards a new sports car for the Teacher. Something must have been turning within me.

Finally, as indicated at the beginning, two events broke my connection with the School. First, Robert's claim to have been visited personally by the Absolute, as though the whole universe could fit inside a nutshell. Second, Robert's renewed prediction that California would fall into the sea. I admit I had not previously investigated whether such an event was physically possible, but that Robert hadn't checked either struck me as intellectually lazy. From there the whole fantasy of the Fellowship unravelled as fast as a cat might pull the wool from an unfinished scarf.

A non-member friend suggested that, as I was due to lead a meeting, I take bets on the supposedly impending fall of California. This would certainly have 'created memory.' In the event I decided to let sleeping dogs lie. I withdrew from leading the meeting and failed to show up.

Afterwards two students tried to contact me but I didn't meet them for one reason or another, and a senior student from Apollo sent me a gift which I donated to the charity shop. And that was that.

A REASON FOR NOT BELIEVING ANYTHING I HAVE WRITTEN

As you have read this far, it is likely that you have applied your mind to some of the doubts that a careful study of the fourth way throws up. Even so, someone committed to believing everything at all costs could say that my intellectual part is blinded by its own cleverness, that after all the intellectual centre, being part of the sleeping machine, cannot share the point of view of higher centres.

The fourth way presents us with the paradox that, on the one hand we are asked neither to believe nor disbelieve anything we hear, and that Gurdjieff set out to:

> ...destroy, mercilessly, without any compromises whatsoever, in the mentation and feelings of the reader, the beliefs and views, by centuries rooted in him, about everything existing in the world[115]

---

[115] Gurdjieff, preface to *Beelzebub's Tales to his Grandson*

...and on the other hand, that the fourth way carries with it a huge baggage of material which must be taken on faith.

Leaving aside everything unverified and unverifiable, I do not deny the possibility of living a life more free from inner torment, a state of clean awareness from which we could go about our everyday tasks with more joy.

THE BURNING OF PARADISE

Robert used to tell us that there were 30,000 conscious beings in the universe. He based this on the omen that the town of Paradise not far from Apollo had a population of 30,000. It is a peculiarity of Robert's interpretation of omens that the almost total destruction of Paradise by fire in 2018 did not result in any revelation that 'higher forces' were trying to tell him that something was not right in the school.

I ABANDON THE SYSTEM

I abandon the System
—P. D. Ouspensky[116]

Towards the end of my time in the Fellowship I came across the term *apophenia*. The Merriam-Webster dictionary defines apophenia as "the tendency to perceive a connection or meaningful pattern between unrelated or random things." I was in any case aware of the idea. I had read somewhere that Sigmund Freud became convinced that he would die at age 62 because he kept seeing the number 62, just as I became accustomed to seeing the number 44. (Sigmund Freud actually lived to age 83.)

As a sense of doubt crept up on me I looked out for the number 44, feeling that if the ascended spiritual essences of past conscious beings were real they would surely send me confirmatory messages. If I looked at the time and it happened to be (say) 2:44 this I would take as confirmation.

---

[116] Quoted in Rodney Collin, *The Theory of Conscious Harmony* p.179

But clearly just one confirmation was not enough. I began to wonder why Influence C were limited to such tiny adjustments in the material world.

After I had already decided to leave, I did receive confirmation in the number plate of a car driving just ahead of me. It read, CA11 TME, 'call time.' Enough is enough.

Ouspensky himself abandoned the teaching he had so painstakingly reconstructed from Gurdjieff's sometimes obscure presentation. At the end of his life he "became decisive, calling the meetings in London that were to confuse and alienate so many of his followers, at which he abandoned the system, refusing to respond to any of the old 'system' language and speaking with even greater enigmatic brevity than he had used in New York."[117]

Ouspensky said, "People only must know to some extent what they want and must have courage. Courage to experiment. Get material from people. From this material, real facts, real questions, we begin to reconstruct. ... Something changed for you. You have got something. ... System as I learned it was Gurdjieff's. But what you can understand in your own experience is yours. No-one can take it from you. From this you can reconstruct."[118]

Opinions diverge on whether at the end of his life Ouspensky was broken and disillusioned or whether he underwent a miraculous final transformation. Either way, it is difficult to interpret what he said as an invitation to continue with the System as presented in In Search of the Miraculous (which ironically was published after his death, when he had already abandoned it).

---

[117] Beckwith p.34. Ouspensky's last meetings as recorded in A record of meetings don't necessarily suggest that he 'became decisive.' "Miss B. How can one find harmony? [Miss Q. repeats the question.] Mr O. [to Miss Q.] This is your question? [No reply.] This is my question now, and I have no answer." p. 608.

[118] Last Remembrances of a Magician, as quoted in Beckwith p.38

If I start from where I am, what do I have?

I abandon any idea that there is an Ark of people who will potentially be saved from some coming catastrophe.

I abandon the idea that I am on my eighth lifetime and will become 'immortal within the limits of the solar system' in my next life, or indeed in this one.

I abandon any idea that I am special in any way, that I am superior in any way to anyone else. Any nobility that I may have is only in each action I perform, each word I say or refrain from saying. I am as good as what I do now.

Self-remembering is a method, and probably not the only method, of coming into the present moment, being present with one's whole self. I can, if I try, be centred instead of scattered, less subject to my immediate reactions, more in control. I can, if I try, step back from drowning in the preoccupation of the moment.

It is not a panacea. I have previously explained how it is possible to self-remember, to find a tranquil place within, and at the same time be unwittingly in a dream of spiritual superiority, oblivious of the state of someone sitting next to me. External consideration, the consideration of the needs of others, requires efforts of its own. The idea of external consideration goes back to Jesus and probably beyond.[119] In the Fellowship external consideration seemed not to be applied to life people, people not in the cult. I abandon cults.

There are other ideas in the Work worth considering, although they are not exclusive to the fourth way. The idea of non-expression of negative emotions is at the very least worthy of careful consideration, even though it may be argued that perhaps there are times when it is appropriate to let anger out (I do not say so, I merely assert the possibility). Not judging goes back at least as far as Jesus.[120] The idea of 'things as they are, myself as I am' and efforts to connect

---

[119] Matthew 5:44

[120] Matthew 7:1

with the present moment have considerable merit. In the book *The Power of Now*, Eckhart Tolle gives a thorough account of why living in the present moment is a good thing. We can live more efficiently and more joyfully if we stop living predominantly in the past or the future, and become less burdened by unnecessary preoccupations.

The reward of presence is in the present. Can I practise it without being special or having to believe unverifiable things about the cosmos? Why not? Believing I am special is another illusion.

The idea of the many 'I's is also worth serious consideration. As I have said already, the idea that we are multiple goes back to the Ancient Greeks, an idea that is now more-or-less mainstream in modern psychology. There is even an approach in psychotherapy based on it, *Internal Family Systems*, in which a calm self can emerge from gradually resolving the conflicts between what are called 'parts' of a person.

Perhaps with a little effort to be more present, to pause between action and reaction, and if necessary also with some healing work, it may be possible to achieve the not inconsiderable joy of being our ordinary selves. As for the metaphysical apparatus of the fourth way—its ray of creation, its higher hydrogens, the crystallisation of higher being bodies, the vanishing promise of immortality within the limits of the solar system, and its non-existent men numbers 5 to 7—there is no reason to believe it true.

THE SUNK COSTS FALLACY

Someone suggested on the FoF discussion forum that people may stay in the Fellowship because of the sunk costs fallacy. The sunk costs fallacy is the idea that one should stick with a thing even when it is failing, so as not to waste the money and time one has already invested in it.

On a personal scale, I am sometimes tempted to drink wine even when I have decided to have an alcohol-free day, simply because there is some left in the bottle from the previous day and I do not want to see it wasted. Wine after all costs money. Of course if I drink the wine (or left-over food for that matter) that I don't need, it is just as much wasted as if I had thrown it away.

Perhaps there are those in the Fellowship who have spent not only considerable sums of money but also many years of their lives on a project to achieve awakening—higher states of consciousness. Perhaps they want to continue to believe, because the alternative is to feel that they have wasted their time.

To those people I would say two things. First of all, as the saying goes, today is the first day of the rest of your life. There is nothing stopping you being present now. Presence is not a project for the future. The second thing is that not everything was an error, and there is something useful that you can take away. Strip away the error and keep what you now know. Even Burton has said it is fine to make mistakes, but try not to repeat them (being in a cult and believing un-evidenced statements is of course one of the mistakes not to repeat).

When I decided to leave the School I was reminded of the song *Teo Torriatte* by Queen, which for some reason I found quite emotional. It contains the line:

> In the quiet of the night let our candle always burn, let us never lose the lessons we have learned.

BE ORDINARY

I will try, like them, to be my own silence: and this is difficult.
—Thomas Merton[121]

Early on in my encounter with SES I came across the idea that because we are identified with the many 'I's (SES called them 'ideas'), we believe ourselves to be them and we are therefore not in touch with our real self (which SES called *the Self* or *Atman*). I thought (in Fellowship terms, I had an I, or as Gurdjieff might have put it, 'it was thinking in me'), if I am not me, who am I? I felt myself to be working to abolish myself so that somehow real self could emerge. I imagined 'me' on one side of a veil and real self as something else on the other side.

The fourth way puts this slightly differently. We are machines who, variously, either do not have souls and have to create them through our 'conscious labours and voluntary sufferings,' or else we have souls ('higher centres') that are dormant. Loosely, we are not in touch with our higher centres (whatever they may be).

In Grimm's fairytale *Maid Maleen*, the prince rides by but he cannot hear Maid Maleen because she is locked in a stone tower. On the one hand, the stone tower has saved her from the destruction that has been visited on the kingdom, and on the other hand it is a prison which blocks her from a full life. One might interpret the stone tower as personality, the mask we wear to protect us from all those who would hurt us. Yet it is precisely this that also prevents us from attaining our full potential as human beings and stops us loving and living authentically. (I am not suggesting that this is the only possible interpretation of the fairytale, nor that fairytales necessarily must have psychological interpretations.)

---

121 Thomas Merton's poem, In Silence

If I take myself to be the mask and the mask is not the real self, then from the point of view of the mask it does have to abolish itself in order that real self can come into being. But the idea that I have to abolish myself arises from the idea that I am the mask, which is false.

The solution to this conundrum is simply to be present. The mask is my imaginary picture of myself which I not only believe to be me but also try to persuade others is real (although others are less likely to be fooled than I am). In the present moment, if I simply allow myself to be present, treating all opinions about myself as merely provisional, and being willing to allow things to be what they are and others to be who they are, then there is some possibility of clarity.

I used to think of this as abolishing the homunculus, the story I tell to myself about myself. I don't know what the homunculus is supposed to represent in alchemy but to me it was my little imaginary picture of myself, something that perhaps no-one else believed in, or at any rate not in the way I did.

In SES someone referred to 'peeling away the skins of the onion.' At the time this puzzled me, because anyone who knows about onions will know that once you have peeled away all the skins there is nothing left. The onion consists of its skins. I think now that was the point.

We are made of stories. We change throughout our lives (it is something of a tragedy if we can't), not only changing in our bodies but also in our beliefs, our way of being, and our relationships with others. We live in different houses, sometimes even different countries, wear different clothes, like different music, have different friends.

It is possible with practice to live from the moment of awareness instead of from what we imagine to be the case and our opinions about it. It is another question whether those opinions are right or not. They are so many interesting fishes in a pond. We can learn to be more adaptable.

No doubt there are different levels of ordinary consciousness, and one can be free or less free of various preoccupations and tormenting thoughts. But if there is a higher state of consciousness it is probable that it would be a state of more clarity rather than anything weird.

From Ibn Al-'Arabi, quoting Nunah Fatima Bint Ibn Al-Muthanna, a Sufi woman in Andalusia:

"I, together with two of my companions, built a hut of reeds for her to live in. She used to say, 'Of those who come to see me, I admire none more than Ibn Al-'Arabi.' On being asked the reason for this she replied, 'The rest of you come to me with part of yourselves, leaving the other part of you occupied with your other concerns, while Ibn al-'Arabi is a consolation to me, for he comes to me with all of himself. When he rises up it is with all of himself and when he sits it is with his whole self, leaving nothing of himself elsewhere. That is how it should be on the Way.'"[122]

The Vedanta claims that consciousness does not arise from matter, but rather the brain is a channel through which the universal consciousness passes. As I have argued previously, there is no obvious way of testing this, one way or the other. Let us then accept that we don't know. It makes little difference to anything practical, because to connect with any universal consciousness we would need to be present to our lives now.

To be a beginner

One of my favourite quotations, towards the end of my time in the Fellowship, was Goethe's advice that we should do well to remain as wise in later life as we were when we were twenty:

"People always fancy," said Goethe, laughing, "that we must become old to become wise; but, in truth, as years advance, it is hard to keep

---

122 Sufis of Andalusia p.143

ourselves *as wise as we were. Man becomes, indeed, in the different stages of his life, a different being; but he cannot say that he is a better one, and, in certain matters, he is as likely to be right in his twentieth, as in his sixtieth year."*[123]

and another was Rilke's on being a beginner:

If the Angel deigns to come, it will be because you have convinced him, not with tears, but by your humble decision always to begin: to be a beginner![124]

In some ways I was not a believer at heart but an explorer, a discoverer. But we might say the same of many who subsequently left the Fellowship but who, while in it, assumed without question its fragile belief structure, as I did. We were not as strict as Socrates in knowing that we did not know.

What does it mean to remain as wise as we were when we were twenty? I think it means to know that we do not know and at the same time to have a wide-eyed desire to find out. The difference that experience can make is that we are less gullible.

We shall not cease from exploration
And the end of all our exploring
Will be to arrive where we started
And know the place for the first time.[125]

---

[123] Conversations with Eckermann: 17 February 1831

[124] Si l'Ange daigne venir, ce sera parce que vous l'aurez convaincu, non pas avec des pleurs, mais par votre humble décision de commencer toujours : ein Anfänger zu sein! R. M. Rilke, Lettres françaises à Merline, 1919-1922, Paris, Seuil, coll. « Pierres vives », pp. 37-38.

[125] T. S. Eliot, Four Quartets

Two key issues

I started with two desires: to find out the meaning of life, and to find inner peace, which I conflated with the idea of a higher level of consciousness.

In regard to the first, SES framed the quest for the meaning of life as the desire to find the Truth with a capital 'T.' The problem, though, is that once truth has a capital 'T,' the quest turns into the revelation of a dogma rather than an open-ended enquiry. If the dogma is actually true then it ought to be able to withstand any amount of reasonable criticism. Thus, though the student sits at the feet of the master, the master should tolerate and even welcome the most penetrating and testing of questions, and should be able to say what is opinion and what is well-evidenced, and what the evidence is. All belief should be understood to be provisional.

Whether there is a divinely-ordained meaning to life, or whether meaning is created by us, humanity will need to find common ground in order to avert the catastrophes that threaten us and that we have largely created ourselves. Developing and strengthening ideals of common decency and kindness on both individual and political levels is crucial, and for that, those of us who care should, in the first instance, do our best to behave well in each word and action every moment of each day.

Regarding the search for inner peace, or for clearer states of consciousness, there is no obvious reason why such states depend on the idea that the whole universe is made of consciousness. As pointed out before, it is a matter of debate whether consciousness can arise from matter and it would be even more challenging to show how matter could arise from consciousness. So we can still try out methods of achieving inner calm and clear understanding without any mystical baggage. I think I am right in saying that the ancient Stoics did the same. There is emerging evidence that various techniques for being more in the present moment can promote both inner calm and healing, and such techniques come without any requirement to join a school.

My own experience, such as it is, suggests that part of the secret of inner calm is doing my best to have a clear conscience, being sparing with thoughts and letting the dust settle by coming into the present moment. Very few of our small problems exist in the present.

ON BEING ORDINARY

It is my hope that, by people of good will making continued efforts to be decent human beings, and by making those efforts moment by moment, the ethos of ordinary decency can spread gradually outwards. We have to start from here. As mentioned at the beginning, it is said that we are each connected with anyone else on the planet by at most six handshakes. That is not to say that political activism does not have a place, but the effort to be kind is essential.

Now that I am no longer a potential immortal on my eighth lifetime, and am potential food for worms rather than for the moon, I come back to one of my favourite parts of the Bible, the book of Ecclesiastes.

"Vanity of vanities, all is vanity," it begins. A more modern translation for 'vanity' is 'meaningless.' When I got over the shock of realising that the book of Ecclesiastes was calling everything meaningless I came to accept it, and to understand that my life has as much meaning as I choose to give it, and that is achieved in the details of what I do for myself and my family and for anyone I might have anything to do with.

"Go thy way, eat thy bread with joy, and drink thy wine with a merry heart: for God now accepteth thy works. Let they garments be always white; and let thy head lack no ointment. Live joyfully with the wife whom thou lovest all the days of thy vanity: for that is thy portion in this life, and in thy labour which thou takest under the sun. Whatsoever thy hand findeth to do, do it with thy might; for there is no work, nor *device*, nor knowledge, nor *wisdom in the grave, whither* thou *goest.*"[126]

I don't believe that living well needs to be complicated.

---

[126] *Ecclesiastes 9:7-10*

BIBLIOGRAPHY

Abbreviations of titles as given in the footnotes are given in brackets.

P. D. Ouspensky

A further record, Penguin Arkana 1986
A record of meetings, Penguin Arkana 1992
Conscience, the search for truth, Routledge and Kegan Paul 1979 (Conscience)
In search of the miraculous, Routledge and Kegan Paul 1950
The fourth way, Routledge and Kegan Paul 1957 (Fourth Way)
The psychology of man's possible evolution, Penguin Arcana 1991 (Psychology)

G. I. Gurdjieff

Beelezebub's tales to his grandson, Penguin Arkana 1985 (Beelzebub)
Meetings with remarkable men, Penguin Arkana 1985
Life is only real then, when I am, Routledge and Kegan Paul 1981
Transcripts of Gurdjieff's meetings 1941-1946, Book Studio London 2008

Other works referred to

Beckwith, Gerald de Symons, Ouspensky's Fourth Way, Starnine Media, Oxford 2015 (Beckwith)
Bible: for quotations I have used the King James version.
Burton, Robert Earl, Self remembering, Globe Press Books, New York 1991
Collin, Rodney, The theory of celestial influence, Penguin Arkana 1993
Collin-Smith, Joyce, Call no man master, Gateway Books, Bath 1988 (Collin-Smith)
Ibn 'Arabi, Sufis of Andalusia, Beshara, Cheltenham 2014
Ibn 'Arabi, Whoso Knoweth Himself, Beshara, Oxford 1976
Shushud, Hasan Lutfi, Masters of Wisdom of Central Asia, Inner Traditions, Vermont 2014

The slightly scruffy cat of reason

The rat of woo

Milton Marmalade:
A mermaid in the bath

A mermaid turns up in your bath, without explanation or warning—what do you do? It's almost as disruptive as the search for Truth or (worse) finding it. To complicate matters further, Lionel falls in love with her just before she disappears into the clutches of the evil Dr Squidtentacles.

Lionel's efforts to rescue her are aided by his friend Captain Kipper, the Higgs Bosun and the lovely Lola 'Hotstuff' Tabasco, and complicated by international hallucinogenic chilli dealer Ramón Pimiento el Picante.

This is a ripping yarn with some very slow car chases involving a Morris Minor, and a slow ping-pong duel Matrix-style, not to mention (but I will anyway) a Greek chorus of Cornish villagers, an atomic submarine and a description of St Doris Island and what took place there in the reign of Queen Elizabeth I.

Milton Marmalade's remarkably silly stories for grown-ups

A slim volume of strange tales which struggle with universal questions like the meaning of now, infinity, and why Wolf fell in love with Redcap. The girl who was not a vampire explores the problem and triumph of being who you are. Chocolatina is a satire on the odd puritanism that informs some New Age thinking and at the same time a paean in praise of chocolate. Milton Marmalade has also sneaked in a few poems, mostly silly and one just a little bit erotic (not enough to make you spurt your takeaway coffee in public). In a deliberate protest against the decayed mores of the age, the poems rhyme. A literary tapas time for curly minds everywhere.

Milton Marmalade—'An idiot at the height of his powers.'

For a free story, go to: www.miltonmarmalade.co.uk

A poem from David Henschel's *Heres and Nows*

Enjoy, oh do enjoy
The hereness and the nowness of it.
Whatever is beyond, behind
Be, if you must, aware of
But not too much—no more than serves
To measure by, to savour by
To live by grace within
The here and now.

Heres and Nows

Poems from a life

David Henschel

It is the clumsy man we too much are
That cannot delicately hold the time
Within his juggling mind
And commandeer the chasing heart
Softly to send the blood like fingers
To touch and know the living hour
And store it richly by.

One day we die.
They say we scan
In the last living moments all our span.
We'd wish, I think, to go to Death
Or God
Like guests with gifts
Remembered and collected from our store
Of heres and nows
And say:
This trust of life's fulfilled,
This gift's returned, with more I found:
I was not poor.